Freed to Love

FREED TO LOVE:

Process Interpretation of Redemption

Norman Pittenger

King's College, Cambridge

Other Morehouse-Barlow books by Norman Pittenger

The Ministry of all Christians
Preaching the Gospel
Before the Ending of the Day

Published by

Morehouse-Barlow Co., Inc.
78 Danbury Road
Wilton, Connecticut 06897

Library of Congress Cataloging-in-Publication Data

Pittenger, W. Norman (William Norman), 1905-
Freed to love.

1. Redemption. 2. Church. 3. Lord's Supper.
4. Prayer. 5. Process theology. I. Title.
BT775.P66   1987   234   87-12287

ISBN 0-8192-1404-3

Printed in the United States of America

Contents

Preface

After the publication of my book *The Lure of Divine Love* (Pilgrim Press, New York, and T. and T. Clark, Edinburgh, 1979), I was asked by a number of readers, who were kind enough to write to me or speak to me, about the application of that book's central affirmation—that God is best conceived as Love-in-act or Lover-in-act—to various aspects of Christian faith. Two or three of these were frequently mentioned: What could one say about redemption or salvation in this sort of theology? What could be affirmed about the Christian fellowship, the Church and its worship? and What could be said about prayer and praying if this "Process" context were to be adopted?

In this book I will look at the first of these matters, redemption or salvation; and then say something about the other two (Church and worship and personal praying) in the light of that discussion. But necessarily I begin with an insistence that any responsible theology must be both "appropriate" to the general apostolic witness as found in Scripture and in ongoing Christian experience, and also "intelligible" to men and women today in that it helps to make sense of our contemporary understanding of how things go in the world. I am indebted to my friend Professor Schubert M. Ogden of the Perkins School of Theology in Dallas, Texas, for this way of stating the case. In several recent writings he has argued eloquently and convincingly that any possible theology today must be exactly that: "appropriate" and "intelligible."

This opening chapter is followed by a summary, altogether too brief but I hope not inadequate, of how redemption or salvation has been understood and interpreted in earlier centuries of the Christian tradition. Then I discuss a way in which, as I see it, this experience of deliverance (which I urge is our being "freed to love"), may best be presented today. That chapter is the core of the book. It leads naturally to a consideration of the place of the Cross in the total picture, with some treatment of the themes of "justification" and "sanctification," which have played so large a part in traditional thought in Christian circles. Something is then said about the important (and today pressing) issue of the divine working towards freedom in love, outside and apart from, as well as within, the Christian tradition.

Since in our day there has been much stress on what has come to be called "liberation theology," a succeeding chapter takes up this theme and its relationship with redemption or salvation in a more personal sense. There follow chapters on the Christian fellowship as the "loving community" where such freedom is known, and on eucharistic worship—the Lord's Supper or Holy Communion—as the chief expressive action of that community. Finally there is a short chapter on prayer, interpreted as the intentional act where believers "attend" to the divine Love and Lover—who is indeed everywhere present and active (but not always seen and given concentrated "attention") and thus evokes an appropriate response from the believer. To attend to God in that focal fashion is to realize in one's inner life the reality of the *divine* Love which frees human life to be expressed in *human* loving.

The chapters on the Church and the eucharist are revisions of essays which have appeared in the *Epworth Review*, published in London by the Methodist Church of England. This material has been considerably altered to make it fit in with the main theme of the present book.

I am grateful to the kind persons who have written to me or spoken to me about the earlier book mentioned at the beginning of this preface. Thanks to their encouragement I have ventured upon this one, in the hope that it may be of some assistance to them by showing that the perspective of Process Thought is enormously useful in the highly important enterprise of re-conceiving the tradition of faith, worship and life, which we have received from our fathers and mothers in the Christian community. As always, I owe much to conversations with friends and colleagues in the Faculty of Divinity of the University of Cambridge, of which I have the privilege of being a member; and also to those in King's College with whom I am daily associated. These last have made my quarter-century in Cambridge both pleasant and rewarding.

Norman Pittenger

King's College,
Cambridge, England.

1

Appropriate and Intelligible Theologizing

Central to the continuing life and experience of the Christian community is a sense of deliverance from human wrong and an establishment of right and fulfilling relationship with God. Sometimes this has been referred to as redemption, sometimes as salvation, sometimes as reconciliation, sometimes as atonement. Whatever term may be used, Christians have been convinced that in some fashion God has provided in Jesus Christ a way in which human life may be renewed, enhanced, given meaning and made right. Without such a conviction the identity of the Christian tradition would be lost.

Furthermore, this experience (if that is the correct word for it) has been the basis of all theological interpretations of the significance of Jesus Christ; what has traditionally been styled his "work" has been the grounds for what is said about his "person." To put this in conventional theological language, soteriology has been the presupposition for christology even when "textbook" theology has reversed this order. There can be no doubt that christology has been directly related to what Christians have believed about God's nature *and* about God's "salvific" activity in the world.

But in our own day a difficulty has become increasingly obvious. While the sense of deliverance has been constant and central, the commonly accepted traditional interpretations of that reality have been less appealing and indeed have often seemed both meaningless and "sub-Christian." As a consequence, many good people within the Christian churches, and vast numbers of people outside them, have been prepared to dismiss the whole matter as irrelevant. They have found many of the commonly accepted interpretations to be without experiential backing and have been led often to wonder what, if anything, could be meant when there is talk of deliverance or redemption through Jesus Christ.

I suggest any possible interpretation which can make sense for and appeal to our contemporaries must be both *appropriate* to the Christian tradition as a whole, (with its origins in the events to which the New Testament bears specific witness), and also *intelligible*: understandable in the light of our present knowledge and relevant to the situations in which men and women actually find themselves. In his recent book *The Point of Christology* (SCM Press, 1982), Professor Schubert Ogden uses these two terms—appropriateness and intelligibility—and in an earlier work *Faith and Freedom* (Christian Journals Press, 1979) he did the same but with a more extended discussion. I am indebted to Professor Ogden for making quite plain the importance of both of these. I also agree with him that New Testament study has greatly helped us to grasp what in fact *is* appropriate, while the Process conceptuality (to which both he and I happily subscribe) is helpful in enabling us to work out a position which is also intelligible to our contemporaries.

Before I endeavor to spell out what is involved in speaking of appropriateness and intelligibility, I must make a few preliminary remarks.

First, I am by now I suppose a very "senior theologian," since for more than a half-century I have been engaged in studying, teaching, lecturing and writing about matters of theological import. For this reason I am sufficiently aware of the theological fads and fashions which have come and gone over the years and I have shared the various enthusiasms and profited from the various emphases in the theological world during those many years.

But secondly, I have become more and more convinced over this period that Process conceptuality is the best one available to us today for the never-ending task of "re-conceiving" the Christian witness and the faith to which that witness testifies. I have already argued for this conceptuality, in several books, including most recently *The Lure of Divine Love* (T. and T. Clark, 1979) and *Picturing God* (SCM Press, 1982). Later on in the present book I shall note the main emphases in "Process Theology"—a term which I do not like much but which has become popular. But now I wish to speak at greater length of the necessity of appropriateness and intelligibility to whatever may be the particular kind of theologizing in which one engages. (This will prepare us for the following discussion of deliverance or redemption.)

I believe there are three essential elements in "appropriateness" and three significant points in "intelligibility" or (as I often like to call it) "availability." There are also dangers which a too-strong emphasis on one or the other of these, when adopted without criticism, is all too likely to entail.

Professor Ogden speaks of appropriateness as a matter of fidelity to the general primitive apostolic "witness" and I agree with him. However, it seems to me that there is more to be said.

Theology is appropriate (1) when it reflects in some genuine fashion the earliest Christian presentation of the originating event of Jesus Christ; (2) when it seeks to be loyal to the ongoing and living tradition of the Christian community as this community has developed through the centuries following that originating event; and (3) when it can be validated from what we might style the constant Christian experience of worship, prayer and discipleship. Any such listing demands that we attend to the actual situation in respect to each of these aspects. The mere listing of them is not enough; we need to come to an understanding of what each of them means.

To talk of fidelity to the apostolic witness is to point to the biblical grounding for the theologian's task. Above all, it is to say something about Jesus Christ, his life, his teaching, his work, and everything else that can be included when we name that historic event. But we do not possess the kind of information which would make possible a clear and unambiguous appeal to historical data about Jesus. The days of the "quest for the historical Jesus" are over and done with, both in the older sense and in the more recent attempts by German scholars. New Testament scholarship is not able to recover for us a clear picture of Jesus, his teaching, his actions, and his own sense of vocation, of the kind which for centuries it was assumed was possible. Nor can it give us a certain and secure account of his supposed response to the divine imperative, such as the "new questers" have sought to portray. That there was an historical basis, in a life actually lived out in Palestine, is not in question. Nobody competent in the field is these days so silly as to subscribe to the "Christ-myth" theory of an earlier day; although fairly recently a scholar in a quite different field (in Germanic studies, I believe) produced an amateur book in which he thought to show that it was possible to revive that theory. The point here is not whether there was an historical Jesus who actually existed in Palestine, but how it is that we learn about him. What is more, even if some such historical portrayal were in fact given to us to know, there remains what Dennis Nineham has called the strangeness of the story. This Jesus was an inhabitant of a world of ideas, attitudes, beliefs and views about things which is not our world. He was a Jew, nurtured in Jewish religious beliefs and practices, accepting (as was inevitable at the time) the patterns of thought that were then prevalent. Whatever may have been original in his understanding of these matters, he simply cannot be removed from his own time and place and brought into our day in such a fashion that he is made to think and speak as we should do. Years ago, Professor H. J. Cadbury rightly warned against "modernizing Jesus."

What we have in the New Testament (for an understanding of which the Old Testament is enormously important, since it provides the material from which New Testament thought developed) is the faith-witness as I call it, to the deep impact or impression made upon very early members of the Christian community by the reports about this man. The stories told about him, as well as the accounts of his teaching, were inevitably colored by the response to that impact which was present in the early community of Christian believers. It would be absurd to think that we can get "behind" their witness, although it is perhaps possible that what Willi Marxsen has spoken of as "a canon within the canon" may bring us closer to the actual events. Essentially, however, the witness with which we have to do is the total New Testament picture, told us *from* the stance of primitive Christian belief, so that it might awaken others *to* share that faith. In the Pauline phrase, it is given "from faith to faith." It was directed to those who heard what was being proclaimed in those days and whose response was invited to what was thus proclaimed.

There is a corollary here. The purpose of the apostolic witness as a whole is to point to the event of Jesus Christ as the human enactment (in the world of historical occurrence) of the God who was the God of Israel. For the first Christian community this God of Israel was *also* the deity about whom non-Jewish religion and philosophy, as for example in Greek circles, was somehow concerned. In this given event, whose historical reality was taken for granted, this one God was believed to have acted humanly, "in a man," so that there was given a *human* disclosure of the *divine* nature and activity. Not only was God shown to be "like that"; God was believed to be actively present there, yet actively and savingly present in a genuine and entirely *human* existence. God was revealed to be sheer Love, both in his nature and in his action. God was not only revealed there, however, God was also releasing into the world the same Love-in-act which is his innermost quality, and which delivers men and women from wrong, sin and loneliness.

Thus the requirement of fidelity to the apostolic witness is at the same time the requirement that anything and everything said about God shall be congruous with, a consequence of, or a necessary implication from, the affirmation that God, the God who was declared to have been humanly enacted and humanly the source of "life in Christ," is nothing other than, as Dante wrote, "the Love that moves the sun and other stars." Furthermore, this Love was portrayed as able to move men and women to respond in their creaturely loving to the divine Love, which was prevenient to that response and which was able to awaken in such men and women, that same heartfelt response.

But the witness borne in the New Testament material does not stand alone. There is also the ongoing Christian tradition, which can rightly by styled a living social process that has been plowed into history. This tradition is supported by the New Testament material, along with the preparation in the Jewish scriptures that were bound up together with the later material to become the Christian Bible. At one time Bible and tradition were thought to be separable, indeed to be separate. But that time is now long past. Both Protestant and Roman Catholic theologians see the Bible as part of the living tradition, even if it has also been taken as the "normative" (since it was historically the "formative") element in the continuing tradition's existence. This is not an invitation for us to accept anything that the tradition may happen to assert, nor all the practices which have been associated with the community which have continued the tradition in history. But it *is* to affirm that all of us depend willy-nilly upon the tradition, not only for the apostolic witness itself but also for our attempt to interpret what that witness has to tell us. Hence any theologizing which is worth doing must be appropriate not only to the apostolic witness but also to this living tradition in its main emphases and insights. Otherwise we shall be engaged in the pathetic enterprise of "de-historizing" the faith with which theology works in its effort to provide some consistent and coherent account of what that faith means and what it demands.

No responsible theologian begins his work *de novo*, as if there were not two thousand years of Christian life, worship and thought behind him or her. On the other hand, no instructed theologian ought to be content simply to repeat, parrot-like, the exact words and the exact notions which have been used at one time or other in the course of that long development. To do the latter would be to reduce a living tradition to an archaic traditionalism, as if the "last word" on matters of the Christian faith had been said at some particular moment along the line of historical routing with no possibility of modification, deepening understanding, and even of necessary correction.

Good theology, in respect to the Christian interpretation of basic beliefs, ought not to "reek of the contemporaneous." Rather, it should be undertaken with a humble yet critical awareness that we belong in an age-long community of faith into which we have been baptized and in which we stand; and that we should be conscious of the past ages of faith and reverent in the presence of such a "cloud of witnesses" who themselves were dependent upon the apostolic witness and what it had to tell them. Thus I urge that a second element in an appropriate doing of theology is fidelity to the Christian tradition—not slavish repetition, but keen awareness and honest recognition that our fathers in this tradition are to be respected, even if in many ways they are not to be followed in servile fashion.

The third element in appropriateness has to do with the present living witness of the Christian experience of worship, prayer and discipleship. Karl Barth is said to have remarked that any sound theology must be "preachable." Whatever may have been his own personal meaning here, it seems obvious that the enterprise of Christian theology should not be carried on as an academic enterprise remote from and unrelated to the concrete existence of men and women who today worship within the Church, participate in its sacramental observance, say their prayers, and seek to live a responsible Christian life in the world. Obviously, the language which a theologian may use will not be the language which is proper to acts of worship, public or private; neither need it make constant reference to patterns of daily behavior by Christian people. Nonetheless, it is bound up with such things; and one of its obvious tasks is to provide both a context for and an illumination of precisely those contemporary ways of worship, prayer and discipleship. Otherwise it would not really be Christian theology at all, but an almost free-ranging speculation of a philosophical sort.

St. Augustine was intent upon doing his own theological work with such insistent reference to the day-by-day Christian life of his times. He may not have been successful in this; in any event, much of what he had to say is hardly likely to have much appeal or to make sense to us in our own time. At least this is the case with some of the major emphases in his work. His particular interpretation is not the point which I wish to stress, however, but that his intention, no matter how well he realized it in actual fact, was always to think and speak as a practicing Christian believer and to do this for those who were themselves also practicing Christian believers. I am convinced that any theologian who knows his or her business will be concerned to do the same. A speculation which bears no relation to this living experience of Christian men and women is likely to be both arid and misleading. Indeed, I should be prepared to say that a theology which cannot in some sense be prayed and hence which is not appropriate to the worshiping, the praying and the religious experience and activity of those who profess and call themselves Christian, will be a theology which is an irrelevance, however interesting it may be as a piece of academic study or a bit of theoretical speculation.

If I am right in what I have said so far, there are obvious dangers to be avoided. I shall mention them briefly. The appeal to the

primitive apostolic witness can easily be associated with biblical
literalism, in fact with an unintelligent biblicism, which the best
scholarship and also sheer commonsense have shown to be absurd.
One of the perilous aspects of this recurrent temptation to biblicism
is all-too-likely to consist in such a wooden use of biblical images
and ideas that we are likely to miss the main emphasis: the apostolic
witness is ultimately to divine Love-in-act, enacted in the Man Jesus
where it has been disclosed and released. The biblicist is so zealous
in maintaining everything in scripture that he or she may very well
fail to put the emphasis where it belongs. The biblicist may stress
God's sovereignty, for example, in such a way that he or she overlooks
the deeper truth that it is always sovereignty in and as Love.

Again, the necessary fidelity to the main strains of the living
Christian tradition can lead to what earlier I spoke of as *mere* traditionalism, with the result that the ongoing movement is, so to say,
stopped at this or that point, with appeal made to such a moment
as if it constituted final and exhaustive truth. But in a social process
like the Christian tradition, what is significant is not so much a
particular point along the line but rather the direction which is being
taken or the routing which is being followed. In biblical language,
the Holy Spirit may be saying to us new things and in a new way,
yet all the while that Spirit is "taking of the things of Christ and
declaring them unto us." Thoughtless traditionalism is easy and simple;
it provides neat answers, just as biblicism provides neat answers. But
the trouble with neat answers in any area of human experience is
that they are so neat, so apparently simple and precise, that the
vastness of the questions is forgotten. The answers themselves are
of limited application; and when taken so naively, the end-product
is a trivial presentation of the truth. Who can estimate the harm that
has been done in religious and theological discussion, quite as much
as in philosophical thought and other areas, by an acceptance of
Decartes' unfortunate notion that truth consists in "clear and distinct
ideas?" Surely vonHügel and Whitehead were correct in their insistence
that on the contrary, truth is found in that which will certainly have
a vivid and luminous center but will equally certainly shade out into
peripheral shadow and nuance. As Whitehead once remarked, we
ought "always to seek clarity and always distrust it."

There is an equally dangerous possibility when appeal is made to contemporary worship, prayer or devotion, and patterns of behavior. Here we may well be perilously near to the uncritical adulation of the contemporary for its own sake. Or we may become victims of a subjectivism which is as misguided as biblicism and traditionalism. An instance of this has lately appeared in Don Cupitt's writings, especially in his *Taking Leave of God*, where he seems to think that God can properly be interpreted as the entirely subjective ideal which animates our contemporary spiritual life, and talk about deity as seriously "objective" (as genuinely there in the cosmos and behind it, awakening a subjective response but not itself objective reality), is only the unfortunate result of assuming that religion has a metaphysical depth and has to do primarily with what is not human but distinctively divine. To my mind, this position of Cupitt's is reminiscent of the grin which remains when the Cheshire cat has vanished.

To sum up, I should urge that appropriateness entails fidelity to the general apostolic (and hence biblical) witness, to the witness of the living Christian tradition as we have received it, and to the witness of the concrete experience of contemporary Christian people in faith, worship and life. All three are necessary and all three are to be critically understood. The danger comes when any of these is taken in such a fashion that the Bible is made absolute, the tradition is given final status, or contemporary experience is made the only court of appeal.

I now turn to what I take to be the three necessary elements or aspects of intelligibility or availability for our contemporaries. These are the points which are required if theologizing is to have its relevant appeal to men and women today. Without them the theological enterprise is perhaps of historical interest or of academic delight. But the point of a Christian theology is that it shall produce a coherent and consistent statement of what faith is all about, of such a sort that persons of good will may see that it makes sense of and gives sense to their common human experience and observation. In their own ways all great theologians in the past have made some such reference to availability, although the precise fashion in which that has been made has necessarily differed from age to age in the light of the actual knowledge and the concrete grasp of human existence which prevailed in this or that period of history.

For us today I believe that the three elements or aspects which must be given recognition—which indeed must be stressed as essential—are: (1) the acceptance of a view of the world which sees the creation as "in process" (or as evolutionary in nature); (2) due regard for the dignity and responsibility of human agents in that world, with a grasp of the reality of secularization but without succumbing to the error of secularism; and (3) the provision of a place in any general world view or conceptuality for the possibility, if not the certainty, that love or persuasion is central to the cosmic enterprise as a whole.

Presumably everybody (with the exception of the American "creationists" who have tried and failed to get their theories made part of the required teaching of science in schools in some of the states), accepts in principle that our world is an evolving creation. Further, it is commonly accepted that the human race itself is the end-product, to date, of a long series of developments which link us with the primates like the various species of ape. In every area where observation has been possible, the processive nature of things is plain enough. Informed people no longer are likely to think in terms of static, immutable and fixed entities. Physics, in its contemporary expression, talks about energy, about events and about "fields" (rather than about simple "location"), with insistence upon quantum-leaps, indeterminacy or unpredictability, and the like. In still other areas of study, such as psychology, we are familiar with both pattern (or *gestalt*) models, on the one hand, and with developmental interpretations of personality, on the other. The educated public (and also, because of television, radio and popular paperback presentations, less sophisticated people), is cognizant of the fact that ours is a dynamic world. Along with this has come also the awareness that "becoming" is accompanied by a "belonging," which is related to the societal or organic quality which runs through the universe.

Any theology which is to speak intelligibly to our contemporaries must therefore speak in terms which manifest awareness of this state of affairs and which sees faith in the context of this broader picture. In the simplest way of putting it, a theology which makes sense today must be one that has reference to and is relevant for a dynamic or evolutionary and an organic or interrelated interpretation of the world. Most theologians are aware of what I have just been saying. Of course they do not succumb to the silly idea that science must always be given "the final veto." They understand very well that the "religious vision," as we may style it, has something to tell us which is more than, although it cannot be contradictory of, a scientifically valid world-picture. But perhaps not enough has been done to show that precisely this processive and societal world-picture provides data which are theologically significant. For example, in such a world-picture it is meaningless to talk of human nature as if it were an unchanged and unchanging affair, exactly like what our fathers in the faith had in mind when they gave the definition of each human as an "animal substance with a 'rational' nature." Likewise, creation in its wider meaning can no longer have to do with a supposed origin at an historical moment "when the world was created." "Create" has now become a verb used in the present tense and not exclusively in the past tense. Doubtless this will be granted by theologians of all schools; the question is whether they have taken it with sufficient seriousness.

Again, a portrayal of God as intrusive into what we know to be a processive world, by occasional remedial incursions, is hardly defensible. Lately I read what is on the whole an admirable book by a distinguished Roman Catholic thinker, Bishop Christopher Butler. It was astounding to see that he coupled his quite proper insistence on divine creative power, which sustains and makes "new initiatives in that world," with the use of the word "intervention" to describe disclosures of God and particular activities of God, as if there were a "somewhere" from which God intervened and as if special acts ascribed to God (like the signal event of Jesus Christ as a decisive divine action in human history) must be "intrusive" into a world which this very same writer had previously described as being always and everywhere the sphere of divine operation.

I urge that a change in outlook *and* a change of language in this and similar matters is necessary if the theology which we produce is rightly to be related to the world as we know it to be. Only thus can theology be intelligible and available today. I will not elaborate here on what this may suggest about such central religious concerns as the practice of prayer and its purpose or about talk which concerns God's governance of the creation.

My second point has to do with the dignity and responsibility which we now see to be proper to human existence. When Bonhoeffer said that "man is come of age," he did not mean that we are so mature that God is no longer to be in the picture. He was not supporting any proud assertion of complete human independence of the divine reality. But he was insisting that we can no longer "run to Daddy" when things go wrong. We are responsible for what we do and we are responsible for the consequences of what we do. We are in the position of men and women who are aware of responsibility and also must seek to act in such ways as shall express it and take measures which can correct what is within our power to correct. Secularization in this sense is a present fact. It is not something wicked or sinful but a manifestation of the fashion in which human dignity is known and asserted, with the recognition that God treats us as those who have been given that dignity and must assume the responsibility (and the accompanying accountability) which goes with it. This is very different from the kind of secularism which denies altogether the existence and activity of God and settles for a totally human (or entirely naturalistic) interpretation of things.

A theology which will be intelligible today must be aware of this "coming of age," must reckon with it, and must see human existence in its dependence upon God but also in such a fashion that it gets its proper place in our broad understanding. Not all theology in our own time has yet reached this position. Often enough there are hangovers of the idea that men and women are practically slaves and not sons and daughters of God. It is not always seen that the appropriate way to speak to and about people is in an idiom which implies that they have both dignity and responsibility and hence may not be treated as things which God manipulates in mysterious ways, without their free consent and cooperation. "Imagine a religion imposed from without, a virtue taught, not as a measure of self-respect, but as a means of propitiating a repulsive, vainglorious, grasping deity, and purchasing from him, at a varying scale of prices, a certain moderation of temperature through the dark mystery of the future. These words are from *The Diary of Alice James* (ed. by Leon Edel:

Penguin edition 1982, p. 160) and they speak to me with a remarkable validity not only for her own time in the last quarter of the nineteenth century, but also for us today.

Thirdly, a theology which will make sense, a theology which can claim to speak in Christian terms about God, should insist that any world-view must leave room for the possibility, if not indeed the certainty, that persuasion or love is central to the dynamic and structure of the universe. One cannot talk intelligibly about "God in Christ" unless one has a conception of the world which allows a place for such love. This is a truth which cuts both ways. It requires a rejection of the kind of philosophical picture which puts the main emphasis upon sheer force as dominant in every area of the creation; it also requires rejection of the idea that we cannot say anything, save from a specifically Christian position of faith, about how things go in the world. At the same time, however, it requires that our way of presenting Christian conviction shall recognize the difficulty in thus stressing love as central and shall find ways in which precisely that stress may be the controlling factor in the theological enterprise.

There are dangers in each of these three aspects. It is possible to use an evolutionary or processive perspective in such a fashion that "process" becomes "progress." When that happens the tragic side of the world is minimized or forgotten. It is possible so to emphasize the evolutionary view that we are given a kind of "escalator" portrayal of how things go, with the absurd notion that whatever is latest is by definition best. But a processive perspective, rightly grasped, has its ups and downs, its fulfillments and its failures. There is nothing automatic about it. We have no reason to assume that our present situation is the "last word" and hence we cannot succumb to the cheerful optimism which the history of our own time shows to be silly and unrealistic.

Again, emphasis upon human dignity and responsibility has the possible danger that men and women may think, and theologians may imply, that after all there is nothing very wrong about humankind. In other words, it can be so misapplied that the appalling reality of human sin is denied. A friend of mine, quite rightly rejecting the view that there is such a thing as inevitable moral progress in human history, said to me one day: "History is the account of the human discovery

of more and more subtle ways of sinning." He was entirely right about
this, although I felt obliged to add the rider, "It is also the story of
God's finding more suitable and subtle ways of handling human
sinning." But surely any view of human dignity and responsibility,
to stress what is so important today, must at the very same moment
be concerned to point out the way in which that dignity can be
mistakenly portrayed as making men and women "masters of all they
survey." Responsibility, however, can be seriously misinterpreted by
a refusal to see that even the most responsible person can often be
in the wrong—and for that wrong there is equal responsibility; the
results of our choices are as inescapable as is human accountability
for them.

Finally, insistence that any world-view open for Christian use
(and hence able to make sense of Christian faith) must presuppose
a possibility and place for love as central and all-important in the
scheme of things, is always in danger of being turned into senti-
mentalism. It can neglect the presence of evil in the world. It can
be guilty of rosy optimism. It can forget that it is not an easy matter
to see and speak of the controlling reality of love in a creation which
is plainly not a nice place but more like a battlefield in which good
struggles against bad, truth against falsehood, justice against injustice,
and love against hatred.

If what I have been saying is true, it demands that we shall be
both faithful and realistic. When Teilhard de Chardin called the
creation the sphere of "amorization," he was speaking as a devout
and convinced Christian. But perhaps he should have gone on to say
that such amorization (while indeed it is the divine purpose and to
the eye of faith can be discerned as the deepest truth about things)
is not so much an easy option as a divine imperative, at least insofar
as we humans have a part to play in the cosmic adventure.

I have sought to state what to me seem necessary conditions
for theology today. Such theology must be faithful to, even when
honestly critical of, the apostolic witness, the living tradition of the
Christian fellowship, and the contemporary experience of Christian
men and women. It must avoid the dangers of biblicism, traditionalism
and subjectivism, all of which threaten this appeal. At the same time
it must see the situation today as one in which our contemporaries

know their world to be an evolving and processive one, understand the dignity and responsibility which are proper to human existence in and under God, and are at least open to the possibility that the creation is not just matter-in-motion nor an area in which coercion is the only effectual power, but rather is patient of human love-in-act and can also be interpreted as precisely the sphere in which such Love-in-act (now with an upper-case "L") is the nature and name of deity. As Crashaw phrased it, if Christian faith is true, Love must be "sole sovereign Lord." A world which is not open to the sovereignty of that Love-in-act is a world which the theologian should be concerned to show is not the real world at all. But emphasis on these points must also avoid the dangers of cheap optimism, overpretentious claims for our humanity, and sentimental notions of love. Only in the context of "stern love" can deliverance or redemption make sense.

As I have said earlier, in my opinion Process Theology (despite its unfortunate name) stands up well to the requirements for such appropriateness and availability. In chapter 3 I shall outline what I take to be the main points in that conceptuality. But I should not deny for a moment that other ways of doing theology may also meet these requirements and if and when they do I at least must welcome them wholeheartedly and gladly.

For some contemporary examples of non-Process theologies let me mention John Macquarrie's theological contribution, not least in his *Principles of Christian Theology,* and Maurice Wiles's work in several books and especially in his recent *Faith and Mystery.* In the United States there is the suggestive theology of Langdon Gilkey and recently Sally McFague. All these fulfill the requirements I have mentioned. On the other hand, theological systems like those proposed by American conservatives like Donald Bloesch and Carl Henry, in two large books by them that have had a wide circulation, seem to me to fail badly at least in respect to the "intelligibility" test. What was produced during the "death of God" period also fails in respect to the "appropriateness" test, as does the recent writing of Don Cupitt in Britain. The widely read books of the English (and now Canadian) theologian J. I. Packer, who speaks for the conservative evangelical school of thought, seem to fail both on critical awareness of appropriateness and in readiness to see the necessity for intelligibility or availability. In respect to Cupitt's books, I believe that his refusal to recognize the requirement of appropriateness to the apostolic witness and the Christian tradition, as well as the rejection of an ontological conceptuality which makes room for Love-in-act as cosmically grounded and not merely as a factor in human experience, is as serious as the other extreme of conservative evangelicalism in Packer. The work of Process theologians obviously seems to me the most satisfactory, which is why I accept it.

I shall not continue with such a listing of names. I may remark, however, that to me, as (to use my earlier phrase) a very "senior theologian," it appears that increasing attention is indeed being paid by many to both sets of criteria; this gives me hope about the future of the theological enterprise. Furthermore, in many quarters it is now recognized that Christian theology is nothing like so simple an activity as some have thought it to be. Problems are not being evaded—as, for instance, the problem of the kind of use which must be made of what I have styled the apostolic witness and the appeal to the age-long Christian tradition, as well as the way in which the understanding that to speak strongly and with conviction about the centrality of Love in the world at large, quite as much as in human experience, demands that an appropriate general philosophical stance be adopted. As to the last of these, it is increasingly recognized that any speaking about God as Love is bound to be problematic in face of the obvious evil in the world and in human life.

Finally, I suggest that we need to see that Christianity is a development from earliest beginnings in Palestine—a development which means that we are not forced to attempt to live, as indeed we cannot live, in first-century days. During the long centuries of the Christian community's history there have been changes and modifications with new and different insights in response to new knowledge and new conditions. At the same time there has been a specific Christian identity, so that in those very changes, mod-ifications and insights, we can yet speak meaningfully of a Christian way of commitment, a Christian way of worship and prayer, and a Christian way of discipleship in which men and women are freed to love. It is rather similar to the fashion in which the great saints of the past, each of them with his or her own distinctive quality, are recognizably Christian in basic orientation, outlook and behavior. Perhaps this requires of us a position which resembles the one adopted by Catholic Modernism earlier in this century, but without imitation of the particular ideas which were entertained by those thinkers who were so tragically rejected by the hierarchical Church of their time. Certainly to somebody like myself, an avowed supporter and defender of Process Theology, this is a welcome consideration. I hope that others who do not adopt this way of theologizing will also understand my point here, for often without knowing it they too are in the company of just such critical yet devout modernists, whether it is of the Catholic type which I accept, or of some other and perhaps more evangelical sort.

2

Interpretations in the Past

In conventional textbooks of Christian theology, it has been customary to have a chapter on "Christology or the Doctrine of Christ," followed by one on "Soteriology or the Work of Christ." Perhaps the titles I have just given are not always found but there can be no doubt that the order of appearance of the chapters is usually as I have put it. First there is Christology, second there is soteriology. Or, first there is a consideration of the "Person of Christ" and second of "the Work of Christ."

I am convinced that this conventional ordering is wrong. For it is only because of what Christians believe has been done in the event which they indicate when they say "Jesus Christ" that they have been concerned to make assertions about who Jesus Christ is. Of course it may be replied that while this is indeed the way things have taken place in a chronological sense, nonetheless it remains true that logically the first concern must be with the "nature of Christ," since it is only in his being who he is that we can speak meaningfully about what he has done. But to my mind this point is mistaken because it implies metaphysical presuppositions that I am sure are in error. The error is in thinking in terms of "beings" or "entities" or even "natures" and "persons," without seeing that whatever may have been the case in earlier days, it is nonsense in our own day to think in that fashion of "things in themselves." Alfred North Whitehead remarked in a different context, "A thing is what it does." Or, to put the point more directly, the world is not made up of discrete entities which can be understood apart from their "doing." On the contrary, the world is made up of activities, happenings, events or energizing occurrences; these are the realities we know and with which we have to deal.

To speak in this fashion is to subscribe to something like a Process conceptuality, whether that is the specific Process Thought associated with those who like me follow Whitehead and his expositor Charles Hartshorne, or whether it is some other approach that also puts its emphasis on the dynamic quality of the world's constituents. Whichever this may be, the point that I stress in this book is the recognition that to speak of the "person of Christ" *is* to speak of the "work of Christ." If we accept the Christian conviction that somehow *God* is here involved, and if we talk (with the New Testament) of "God in Christ" rather than only of the "manhood" of Christ, then any valid Christology *is* a soteriology. A discussion of who or what the event of Christ means is by necessity a discussion of what has been accomplished in and through that event.

This doing, this accomplishment, has been wrought out in the historical realm, through the agency of a genuinely human existence. Since that is the case, it is inevitable that the significance of the doing must also be understood in terms of human existence. This means an interpretation that is available at any given time for those who are its beneficiaries. In the Church's historical development, not only was God believed to be active in that originative event of Jesus Christ in all its richness and complexity, but there was also the reception of the event's accomplishments by those who made their response to it. And this must inevitably have been understood in a way which was relevant to their actual situation, their way of seeing that situation, and their general view of things at their given time and place and under their particular circumstances. In other words, any discussion of redemption cannot be an abstract affair, unrelated to the concrete experience of those who believe that the originating event has had a decisive significance and has spoken directly to their needs.

In this chapter we shall try to see what it was to which the response to Jesus Christ had relevance. Or, as we might phrase it, *how* did men and women experience and understand themselves and their condition? In what given situation did the event have meaning and in respect to what need was it found to be redemptive? This will involve us in an historical survey that necessarily must be more suggestive than exhaustive. (In the next chapter we shall go on to consider how we, in our own time and place and under the circumstances which we know to be ours, may today give an interpretation—appropriate to *our* situation—of the "saving" character of what was wrought out in the originating event.) To paraphrase some words of my old teacher Leonard Hodgson, the question is: what can for us be the understanding of what happened in and through Jesus Christ, if our predecessors in Christian faith understood it in the way they did?

Every attempt to explain or make sense of what in Jesus Christ has been "determined, dared, and done" (in the fine phrase from Christopher Smart's *Song of David*) rests upon what those who offer the explanation regard as the concrete situation or condition from which they believe they have been "delivered" through that event—the event to which they appeal as the effectual cause of such deliverance. So we can say that for them and for everybody redemption is *from* what each age, even each person, considers the basic existential problem: what is responsible for their needy circumstances and what is wrong about them and in them. For them this redemption takes place *to or towards* a new and proper human existence into which they believe they have been brought. It is inevitable therefore that they will speak and write about their salvation, redemption or deliverance in a fashion that has reference to and is relevant for precisely that double experience: "*from* darkness *to* light," "*from* error *to* truth," and "*from* bondage *to* freedom." I hope that the following discussion will support this thesis.

First I shall list the several main understandings of "what is wrong," as I have put it, and what thanks to Christ "has now become right."

1. *From* possession or control by demonic powers *to* realization of the power of God in human existence, made available through God in Christ as one victorious over Satan and his hosts: Christ the victor over the demons.

2. *From* bondage to external influences and human sin *to* "the glorious liberty of the children of God," given through God's action in Christ: Christ the emancipator from slavery.

3. *From* life in violation of divine law (not so much sheer legalism as the will of God revealed to Moses and his interpreters) *to* release

from such a condition into obedience to God's loving expectations, through Christ's identification with the human lot: Christ our advocate before God.

4. *From* alienation and estrangement from God *to* acceptance by God made possible by Christ's offering of himself to the Father: Christ the perfect sacrifice of mankind to God.

5. *From* the corruption and mortality which mark the human condition *to* "newness of life" and to immortality, through Christ's sharing our human condition and his injecting the divine life into his human brothers and sisters: Christ the life-bringer.

6. *From* inability rightly to honor God and to make proper amends for human wrong *to* the requisite penance, made in God's identification with humankind in Christ and hence in his enablement of men and women to "fulfill the demands of God's honor": Christ the satisfaction for sin.

7. *From* the condition of human lovelessness *to* a human response to divine loving in Christ, seen as prevenient to human love and as acted out on the stage of history in that same Christ: Christ the divinely given lover of humankind.

8. *From* inability to satisfy the divine justice in respect to human sin *to* the provision given in Christ that such justice is indeed satisfied through the full and perfect satisfaction known in Christ: Christ our substitute before God.

9. *From* self-centered life, with little regard either for God or others, *to* God-centered and hence loving existence, through following the example and teaching of Jesus: Christ our great example.

10. *From* a deep sense of human unacceptability before God *to* an acceptance of our human existence as already accepted by God, disclosed in "the new being in Christ," and thus making possible an acceptance of self and others, despite a continuing awareness of human unacceptability: Christ the divine physician.

In all these interpretations, there is a sense of reconciliation with God. All of them have been found useful by given people at given times and places in grasping the deep meaning of the New Testament affirmation that "in Christ God was reconciling the world unto himself."

I realize that I have not exhausted all the ways in which redemption has been interpreted during the long centuries of Christian history. Furthermore, I have jumped from what are essentially ancient or medieval or Reformation views to the suggestions made by liberal Protestantism and by Paul Tillich in our own day. Between these (and before these) there were doubtless other theories that dealt with the matter. But I think that they can all be subsumed under one or other of the positions which have been listed above.

We now consider each of the ten "theories" in more detail and with greater precision.

1. There can be no doubt that during Jesus' days in Palestine it was commonly believed that evil spirits or demons, under their lord Satan who was chief of the demons, infested human life and were responsible for emotional disturbances, physical illness and the other evils by which men and women were afflicted. Neither can there be any doubt that Jesus himself accepted those current notions. Certainly those who belonged to his band of followers, as well as the crowds who flocked to hear him, found in demon-possession an explanation of much that was wrong with the world. The demons had come between God and God's people, distorting and perverting and twisting creation so that it was no longer the creation that God had made for good and in which God's good purposes alone were in control. However the fact that in Palestine such beliefs were prevalent does not require us to think in the same fashion. Nor does the unquestionable acceptance of those beliefs by Jesus himself demand that we should take the same attitude to the origin and spread of wickedness, dis-ease, disease, and the other ills in the world. To do that would be to attempt to live in a time that is not our own. But the reality of these beliefs at that time and for those men and women is plainly apparent.

When Jesus "cast out devils," the current belief was that what was happening was a working among men and women to reestablish God's will for good by defeating the evil powers at work in the world, thereby making it possible for the sons and daughters of the heavenly Father to live in harmony with that Father's will and find for themselves fullness or genuine "abundance of life."

Doubtless those beliefs continued in the earliest days of the specifically Christian community. There are obvious statements or indirect traces of them in all the gospel material, which naturally reflects the *sitz-im-glauben*, the faith-situation, as well as the *sitz-im-denken* and the *sitz-im-leben*, the patterns of thought and the concrete conditions, of the primitive community. In the Pauline epistles, and elsewhere in the New Testament, such notions are also present, although with St. Paul and St. John they were not always stressed as emphatically as were other ideas such as deliverance from legalism and its violation or manumission from slavery. The point which I wish to emphasize is that one of the earliest ways, if not probably *the* earliest way, of interpreting what was accomplished in Jesus was to claim that through him God's children were freed from the control of demons and were given a new capacity to live with and for God. Jesus had vanquished Satan and his hosts. Therefore those who responded with faith to Jesus were no longer the victims of demonic powers but had been released from that condition and were now able to live as "more than conquerors," because they no longer needed to fear, or suffer from, the evil powers which had been running rampant in the world's affairs.

Gustaf Aulen is entirely correct in arguing in his famous book *Christus Victor* that this general view, which he calls "classical," was the predominant if not the only interpretation of Christ's work in the primitive and very early Church. But we may think that he is wrong in assuming that it is still the only possible interpretation and that any other is a mistaken or deviant one.

For our purpose, if we take into account Jewish ways of thinking and speaking, it is important to notice that when Jesus is reported to have said that it was "by the finger [or Spirit] of God" that he "cast out demons" and that *therefore* "the Kingdom of God" had been shown to be effectively present, what he was actually saying was that *God* was there present and was there at work. The Kingdom of God in Jewish belief was not a place but a state of affairs—it was a way of indicating God's "sovereign rule." And where we find the sovereign rule of God, we find God *in* his sovereign rule. In other words, God was the ultimate cause of Jesus' expulsion of the demons. Indeed, we may extend this meaning and say that when Jesus took as the heart of his preaching and teaching the "coming of the Kingdom of God," he was asserting that God himself had come "upon" those who could read "the signs of the times" and had delivered his children from demonic agencies in the world.

2 and 3. While St. Paul uses the idea of demons and their defeat
as one theme in his Christian thinking, he tends to put the main stress
on what in my listing are the second and third ways of interpreting
what was accomplished in Christ. This is so obvious that I need not
dwell at length on the point. Men and women who had felt themselves
to be "in bondage" to and hence "slaves" of both sin and the "powers
of this world," had in Christ been set free. Like freed slaves in the
Roman Empire, they had experienced manumission. They had been
given liberty from servitude both to sin and to worldly powers. Now
they were possessed of genuine liberty because they had been adopted
as God's own children. Or, again, using now the image of the law
court, they had been declared "not guilty" by God, because Jesus Christ
had been their advocate and defender—a view which is also found
in St. John's writings and which must have been a fairly widely
accepted position in the primitive days of the Christian fellowship.
Nor can we forget that the two following ideas (sacrifice and "new
life") were also present in these New Testament writers.

For those who themselves had been actual slaves, or had known
what others had experienced through slavery, the interpretation of
deliverance through Christ in terms of manumission made very good
sense. So also, those who were aware of the relief and release which
came when they had been found "not guilty," and had been "acquitted"
after trial in a court of law for supposed illegal or criminal conduct,
would find good sense in a view that through Christ God had "acquitted" men and women and had given them a new status in society
through such acquittal.

4. Many in the ancient world were accustomed to think in terms
of sacrifices offered to God in religious ceremonies, not least in the
Jewish sacrifices in the Temple in Jerusalem and in the long history
behind them. For non-Jews who were well acquainted with sacrifical
rites taken as a way of appeasing pagan deities, sacrificial interpretations of Christ's work also had a particular appeal. The Epistle to
the Hebrews—a tractate by an unknown author and not of course
by St. Paul—is a vigorous statement of such a view. "The blood of
bulls and of goats" could not win God's favor. But what the 1662-63
English Prayer Book called "the full, perfect, and sufficient sacrifice"
which Christ had made to the Father, and into whose benefits those

who believed in him had been taken, was exactly what was required. Jesus had offered himself to the Father; he had surrendered himself utterly to the Father's will to the point of death itself. This self-offering of Jesus God would accept and God had accepted. Those who were faithful to their Lord, in whom God himself had been actively present as in "a Son," were caught up into that same offering on Calvary. It was an offering which both summed up and expressed vividly and finally a total life given in self-surrender. Thus such persons could believe themselves to have been delivered by the sacrifice of Christ from all that impeded their proper filial relation to their Creator, who was now seen also to be their Redeemer in a very specific and enabling fashion.

5. As the Christian gospel made its appeal to Gentiles, and more especially to those who had been influenced by Hellenistic thought (with its background in Platonizing philosophy and in the mystery religions which flourished in the Roman Empire a century or more after Christ), another way of understanding the meaning of redemption became significant. People who shared this background felt that the twin facts of human corruption and mortality were so appalling that release must be sought and that it could be found through a relationship with what was itself incorruptible and immortal—that is, with the divine reality which in their view could not know suffering or death but which remained immutable, impassible, and absolutely perfect in all respects. If in the event of Jesus Christ this ultimate eternal and complete perfection had been made visible and available; if indeed "God had become man," so that human existence might be "divinized;" then it would seem appropriate to say that redemption was a wonderful sharing in incorruptible, immortal, and perfect being. So it is not surprising that the work of Christ was interpreted as precisely the gift of such qualities. Human existence now had been made a participant in the divine reality through the activity of the *Logos* or Word, who was the creative agency in the creation and who, incarnate in Jesus Christ, was able to provide for those who were incorporated into him just such perfection, deliverance from the experience of corruption, and a share in immortal existence.

At the same time, however, many of the older ideas still persisted. Even the philosophically minded Cappadocian Fathers spoke in terms

of possession by Satan and deliverance through Christ from Satan's
control. They even used extraordinary images such as "mousetrap"
or "bait," whereby the chief demonic power was fooled into thinking
that because he had managed to secure the death of Jesus he had
completely defeated him. The real truth was that Satan himself had
been caught in his own devices, because God had given *Jesus* victory
through his resurrection from the dead.

6. There was never any *official* doctrine of redemption, of course.
Although the significance of the *person* of Christ had been defined
in the dogmatic pronouncements which culminated at Chalcedon in
A.D. 451, various ways of understanding "atonement" were possible.
Because there was no officially stated position on how salvation had
been accomplished, these differing ideas could still be propounded
and win acceptance. But with the coming of the Middle Ages, philosophical theologians began again to wrestle with the question. In St.
Anselm we have the enunciation of a theory which presupposed the
penitential system of the Church, which by now had been fairly well
established. It is a mistake to look at Anselm's teaching as based upon
the feudal system, as many historians of doctrine have sought to do.
On the contrary, the view which Anselm put forward in his notable
work *Cur Deus Homo* ("Why God Became Man") must be seen as a
way of affirming that what no human could manage—perfection in
penitence for sin, since human frailty was not competent to make
proper amends for violation of the divine honor which human sin
had tragically offended—God himself had performed in his incarnate
Son. God had "become man" so that full and proper penance might
be offered. God in Man alone could offer this, and the divine honor
could be vindicated only by God's own act in manhood. Hence the
situation to which Christ came and from which humanity was delivered
was one of utter human inadequacy and imperfection, felt seriously
by those who like Anselm knew (in his own words) "the gravity of
sin" and who were humbly aware of their own incompetence to do
what was required to overcome and make reparation for human
sinfulness and human wrong.

7. We come now to a way of thinking which is more appealing
to our own modern minds. This is to be found in the writing of
Abelard. This brilliant scholar, whose life had been tragically affected

by his own experience in love, was greatly offended by what seemed to him to be the abstract and almost mechanical fashion in which Anselm's position was stated. In his commentary on Romans, Abelard offered his own view. Grave injustice has been done to Abelard both by his critics and by his defenders who have talked about his position as "exemplarism" or the "moral influence" theory. A typical instance from a critic is this description from an article by James Atkinson in the S.C.M. *Dictionary of Christian Theology.* "The moral and exemplary character of Christ's love and self-surrender [stirred] the imagination and will be repentance and holiness." So Atkinson describes Abelard's position. In the days of liberal theology Hastings Rashdall, in his great historical study *Atonement*, writes favorably of Abelard but also succumbs to this mistaken reading. He commends Abelard for teaching what he calls a "moral influence" view. But the facts are quite different, as I pointed out nearly forty years ago in "A Note on Abelard" in *The Anglican Theological Review* for October 1946.

What Abelard really said was that in Christ God had acted in sheer love towards sinful mankind. That divine love awakened a response, to be sure, but the response was made not to a splendid human example, but to a vivid disclosure of God's own nature and purpose for God's human children. What is more important, Abelard believed that men and women were caught up in the divine love expressed and enacted in Jesus Christ, with the result that they were enabled to participate in their Lord's anguish, to share in his suffering, and to triumph with him in his resurrection. This last point—participation of the believer in Christ—is beautifully stated in one of the hymns which Abelard wrote for his beloved Heloise when she was the superior of a women's convent. A reading of that hymn, "Alone thou goest forth to die," in terms of what the translator gratuitously assumed to be an "exemplarist" view, led him to produce a sadly erroneous version of Abelard's actual writing. The hymn asks that we be made sharers in Christ's anguish and therefore participants in his victory. The Latin verb is *compatior*, which means "to suffer with." Yet the translator used these misleading English words: "Teach us to *pity* thee, O Lord." Certainly this was the last thing which Abelard intended.

Abelard's difficulty, as I shall urge in the next chapter, was that he did not have available what we might style an ontology which was capable of providing a context for his deep insight. But he was quite clear in his insistence that God had acted in Christ, that this act was a doing by and a disclosure of divine love, and that deliverance from sin was precisely the catching up of manhood, in each and every instance of human response, into that same love. Here was no mere "moral influence" or the imitation of a "godly example"; rather, here was a sharing in the active love that is God himself. For Abelard this was obviously relevant to our human situation as loveless creatures.

8. Still another way of interpreting Christ's saving work was stated later by Grotius and others who followed a juridical line of thought. This view has been popular in evangelical circles where there is much talk about a "substitutionary atonement," with special stress on the "satisfaction of divine justice" found in Christ. Men and women were said to be unable to satisfy that justice, thanks to their appalling sinfulness. They could not fulfill the divine law and they were condemned by God for this utter failure. But God was merciful as well as just; and the divine mercy had a way of handling the situation. God could both be shown to be merciful and at the same time to require a due satisfaction of the justice which was also his nature. In Christ, who was God's Son, the inability of humankind to obey God was met by God's own act in providing a substitute for us. By faith we make our own what God has done both to satisfy this justice and to exhibit the mercy which he entertained towards his erring children.

9. To those who were influenced by the Enlightenment in the eighteenth century and in the years that followed almost up to our own time, such a view seemed barbarous and immorally transactional. The more optimistic understanding of human existence which characterized the post-Enlightenment period, and which was prevalent in the days of what has been styled "old-fashioned liberalism," took a different line. Something was indeed wrong with men and women— and no supporter of that kind of "liberalism" was under any illusions about this sad fact. What was needed, however, was a dedicated following of the teaching of Jesus, in which the divine love was proclaimed and humans were invited to make that love "the master-light

of all their seeing." Since the teaching of Jesus had been acted out
in his own conduct, it was possible for his disciples to imitate him,
to act as he himself acted, and to be inspired by his teaching and
assisted by his example.

Here, if anywhere, we find the sort of interpretation which
Atkinson and others have erroneously attributed to Abelard. For the
"liberals," the trouble with human existence was that men and women
did not have the imagination or the incentive to respond to Jesus'
own example and loyally to follow his straightforward teaching. I have
parodied this on occasion by saying that many thought that what was
needed was more clarity in understanding Jesus' teaching and an
overcoming of the human stupidity which does not see that his
teaching is indeed the only truly human (and divinely endorsed) way
of life. To put it that way is not fair to the liberals; but at least it
gets across something of their way of thinking. Inevitably, that kind
of interpretation had its appeal to men and women who were living
in a much less obviously tragic period of human history.

10. In this all too rapid and brief account, I turn finally to the
suggestion made by Paul Tillich, the nearly contemporary German-
American philosophical theologian who during his lifetime exercised
an enormous influence, especially in North America. Tillich was
deeply impressed by the disclosures of modern psychological inquiry
and he was also much concerned to give an "existentialist" turn to
theological discussion. For these reasons he came to believe that the
basic trouble with men and women is their inability to accept themselves as they are and for what they are. They seek all kinds of escape
routes from such an honest awareness of themselves. In the end, they
simply do not find it possible to live freely; they require that in some
fashion they be enabled to overcome this impossibility by a response
to that which, or to him who, is prepared first of all to accept them
without demanding that they take some prior step to earn or merit
such acceptance. Just here what Tillich called "the new being in Christ"
comes to their aid. In the new event of Jesus Christ, God as "the
ground of being" has shared the human lot exactly as it is; and in
that sharing has demonstrated his acceptance of humanity in its tragic
condition. There God is disclosed as already accepting the unacceptable. And if we are confident that God accepts us just as we

are, we are then able to our turn to accept ourselves—with all our
obvious and appalling unacceptability—and eventually to accept other
persons too, so that in a small way we may become surrogates of
God in his salvific concern.

I believe that Tillich spoke relevantly to modern men and women.
Hence his view not only had an intellectual appeal for them but was
also existentially effectual in bringing them to a realization of their
divinely intended possibility. In a way, Tillich's view was nothing
but a reworking of the old teaching of justification by faith through
grace, which Luther called the *articulus stantis aut cadentis ecclesiae*—
the article of faith of a "standing or falling Church." Tillich was seeking
a modern phrasing for "justification by grace through faith." He found
it by urging that by accepting God's gift in Christ by an act of
continuing commitment men and women were enabled to know that
they can be, and indeed are, delivered from their uncertainties,
insecurities and frustration. They can then discover themselves
enabled to live in a measure of love and charity with their human
brothers and sisters, in and under the divine reality, which for Tillich
was "Being itself" made present in "the new being in Christ." I believe
that what Tillich had to say can be of considerable help to us in our
own attempt to provide a meaningful interpretation of redemption
in Christ.

3

A Contemporary Interpretation

In the preceding chapter I tried to give a short account of the various ways in which during past ages and in the present moment men and women have sought to make sense of what they knew had happened to them as they shared in Christian faith, lived so far as they were able the Christian life, and worshiped God disclosed in Jesus Christ. Each of these ways has been relevant to the kind of understanding of what is wrong in human existence that either prevailed or was largely current in the several different periods. Believers were sure that through the event of Christ they had experienced a "setting-right" of what was basically wrong with them and wrong about them. They naturally sought to interpret this "setting-right" in terms of their own awareness of whatever it may have been that had prevented them from becoming their true and God-intended selves.

So it must be with us. Whatever may have been the case with our Christian predecessors, and indeed whatever may come to be the case with those who will follow us in Christian allegiance, we live today in a particular sort of world and we have our own particular awareness of what is "basically wrong" about us and in us. Furthermore, as Christian men and women, we are convinced that this "wrongness" has been overcome and that in some fashion we have been "set right."

Perhaps we do not think that the *sole* purpose for what occurred in the event of Jesus Christ was our human deliverance. Indeed some of us—and here I include myself—cannot accept the notion of God's action in Christ as being entirely and exclusively directed to human

31

from sin, as it has usually been phrased. Those who
oader view are unhappy with statements such as that
ks of Christ as "a divine rescue expedition." Of course
ᴜᴜᴄ..... e no doubt that one, and in many ways for us a central,
consequence of that event has been human redemption. The Christian centuries cannot have been entirely wrong in this respect,
especially because they all testify to a strong continuing sense of
such redemption by untold numbers of men and women down the
years. Yet it may very well be the Scotist view which makes its
appeal to us.

In the middle ages Duns Scotus was prepared to say that even
if humanity had not fallen into sin (if that is the right way to phrase
it), God would still have crowned and completed his age-long revelatory activity in the world (what some of us would call his unceasing
"incarnating" presence and working) by bringing to a focal expression,
decisively and definitively for us humans, that activity and that
presence in an event such as took place in and around Jesus of
Nazareth. I have put this Scotist view in my own way; but I believe
that I have accurately stated what he had in mind. Certainly it is my
own position. If this is sound, then the redemption of humankind
is indeed of extraordinary importance and for us humans it is of *crucial*
importance; but it must be set in a wider context.

I said at the beginning of this book, and I have repeated in what
has followed, that for me the Process conceptuality provides the most
useful description, of "widest generality" (as Whitehead would have
said), of our world, of ourselves in the world, and of the divine reality
we call God. It is not a substitute for, nor a philosophical expression
of, the affirmations of Christian faith. But it *is* a context or setting
which some of us find invaluable for our theological statement of that
faith. Since this is my own conviction and since I wish in this present
chapter to indicate how to my mind we, today, may best understand
both our human situation and what God has done for us in Jesus Christ,
it will be useful to give a brief (and hence inadequate) outline of this
conceptuality. For a fuller and more satisfactory outline I refer those
who may be interested to the books mentioned earlier and to the
admirable survey by John Cobb and David Griffin called *Process
Theology: An Introduction Exposition* (1977).

The Process conceptuality is a comprehensive world view which begins with an analysis of what it feels like or what it means to be human in a world such as we know our world to be. From that analysis it generalizes, seeking to determine whether such generalization makes sense of and may properly apply to the widest ranges of experience and observation. It finds there is such a correspondence, although inevitably there are rough edges and no claim can be made for absolute finality—how could finite human minds presume to make any such an extravagant claim? In the end, what emerges is something like the following, for which I shall give a number of headings, but without developing them in great detail.

1. Ours is a dynamic and processive world, whose basic constituents are not fixed entities or things but events or occasions, which are objective in their existence but also have a subjective aspect inasmuch as they are the foci of experience (not necessarily conscious experience but nonetheless genuine).

2. In such a world, there is a "becoming" that moves from potentiality, given as an initial possibility, towards actuality or a realization of that potentiality. There is also a "belonging," in that each and every event affects and influences every other event and is itself affected and influenced by those other events. The world and everything in it must be seen as both "a becoming" *and* "a belonging."

3. The divine activity provides initial possibilities, lures towards their acceptance by "prehension" or profound "feeling," seeks for the emergence of novelty or genuine "newness" within the continuing process, and is receptive of what is accomplished or achieved by the several occasions or events as these, in their responding to lure or invitation, "make themselves" or fail to do so.

4. A genuine freedom characterizes the whole creation, but with differing degrees of fullness. Along with this freedom is a capacity to choose from the many possibilities that are available. This means that we do not have to deal with a predetermined movement; on the contrary there is an openness, even a "chance" aspect, in the world. We have no guarantee that everything will go as it should go; there is even the likelihood that, at least in some instances, things will go the "wrong" way.

5. The divine reality—supreme, worshipful, dependable and unsurpassable by any creaturely occasion (although capable of surpassing itself in its later phrases by contributions from the world that it may use and treasure)—is the chief but not the only causative agency. Creatures like men and women (and the other constituents of the world, too) have their own causative efficacy. Thus they contribute, or they fail to contribute, to the creative advance which is the world we know. In contributing to that advance they also make a contribution to God, who is the final recipient as well as the primal cause.

6. God is both the preserver of order and the ultimate source of novelty. God is also the giver of "refreshment and comradeship" (in Whitehead's words), in relation to whom humans, in particular, may serve as "co-creators," thus finding their proper dignity and responsibility. By their being taken into or received by God and made participants in his life, in whatever fashion possible, they "make a difference" to God, especially when such dignity and responsibility are given effectual expression.

In this general context, Christian faith may be expressed. That faith is based upon an apostolic witness which is continued and confirmed in an ongoing social process or living tradition which we call "the Church." Basic to this faith is the affirmation that in the event called Jesus Christ, there is the classical instance of divine disclosure and an effectual operation of God in the human scene. What is *disclosed* is sheer Love-in-act, God's very "nature and name," as Wesley's hymn puts it. What is *operative* is that that same Love-in-act is released into human existence in remarkable fullness and is effectual in providing the "grace" (or divine favor and assistance) that is needed if men and women are to make the right decisions and hence move in the right direction for them, which is towards "the image of God" in humankind. What is thus affirmed in faith or commitment to this event, as God's focal activity (so far as we humans are concerned), is acted out in Christian worship, more particularly in the eucharistic sacrament where believers are convinced that in response to human prayer God makes present the achievement wrought in Christ. And that action takes place in the loving community which both remembers Jesus and knows his Spirit released into human affairs.

I have spoken of the divine *activity*. For some any such talk presents a serious problem. Perhaps they are prepared to say that there is a divine presence which may be known and reverenced; but they are not able to see anything meaningful in our affirming that "God acts." Something must be said about this, if only to make it possible for the reader to grasp the whole position which I am advocating.

Obviously talk about the divine "action" is not literal in nature. It can only be taken as a useful metaphor, drawn from our own human experience and not applied in a wooden fashion to deity. Yet it *is* drawn from our own experience as humans; and we may insist that like all other assertions of such "wide generality," it is entirely legitimate to use that experience as an indication of something about the divine reality about which something must be said, even if always with modesty and with reservations. It is apparent that the world view which I am defending does, in fact, demand that we shall speak of God as active—*God does things*, even if the doing is in many ways mysterious to us.

What then does God "do"—how does God "act"? The answer is that God does not "do" or "act" coercively, by shoving things around or by pushing or pulling them; God's way is always persuasive, as Whitehead (following Plato here, by the way) insisted. So the divine action may be said to be along the following lines (more detailed discussions can be found in the Cobb and Griffin book mentioned above).

First, God "orders" the world so that it may move forward in greater realization or actualization of love-in-action or what Teilhard de Chardin styled "amorization." This is therefore the kind of creation in which such societal process may take place.

Secondly, God gives to each and every event or occasion or agent in the created order its "initial aim," or possibility, which that particular "this or that" may freely decide to act upon as its own.

Thirdly, God continually lures or solicits further development along the lines of genuine fulfillment of possibility, and surrounds each instance with such attractions as may promote exactly that sort of movement forward. However, as we have already seen and know well in our own experience, creaturely freedom may decide negatively rather than positively as to how it will respond to such attractions or lures.

Fourthly, God receives or accepts into the divine nature and life whatever is accomplished or achieved in the creation. To this, God then responds, by using such contributions for further advance. In doing this, God "pours back into the world," as Whitehead once phrased it, what has thus been received into the divine life, so that there may be new occasions and opportunities for the creatures to implement possibility and to fulfill their own "aims." At the same time, they "enrich" God (as I should dare to say) and are to God a cause of delight or joy; on the other hand, their refusal to play their part saddens God and impedes the fullest accomplishment of divine purpose or intention for the creation.

To speak of the divine activity in this fashion is, of course, to reject altogether the common and vulgar notion that the only meaning of activity is the kind of coercive shoving about, pushing or pulling, etc., which, as I noted above, is *not* God's way in the world.

Many of those who have trouble with such talk are victims of the long history in human thought, in which a false disjunction is often found between subjectivity and objectivity. They can understand that we humans behave in an active fashion but they think that it is entirely a matter of human subjectivity, human thinking and human limitation. Or, on the other hand, they may be victims of a highly generalized monistic view, in which anything and everything is "of God," but nothing in particular can be predicated of deity.

The former error confuses our own necessary subjective appreciation with "whatever-it-is," which awakens the subjective response. Whitehead caricatured this be remarking that if such were the case, then it is not the poet (say, Wordsworth) who is "discovered of" or answers to a beauty presented to him; but it is only the poet's own subjectivity. So we should praise not the glory of daffodils but the poet's inner workings which, as it were, creates for itself the notion of their glory. Yet surely all evaluation and appreciation is two-sided; there is that which evokes it and there is the response which is made to that evocative reality.

The latter error mentioned above is a failure to see that only through a particular and vivid event can we come to speak meaningfully of a more pervasive activity in the world. The particular and the universal require each other. This is why I have urged that the event of Jesus Christ is not the supreme anomaly but the "classical instance" that provides a clue or key to that which elsewhere and otherwise is going on.

Of course it may be replied that if God is indeed active, if "God acts in the creation," God must also act in that which is evil—and the age-old "problem of evil" is raised once again. Here I should say with Whitehead that the "limitation of God is his goodness" and that God is not responsible, either directly or permissively, for such evil as is obvious in the creation. I shall not pursue this matter, however, since elsewhere (especially in my book *Cosmic Love and Human Wrong* [Paulist Press, 1978] I have discussed it at length). I may also refer the reader to David Griffin's admirable treatment in his *God, Power, and Evil* (Westminster Press, 1976).

My old teacher Leonard Hodgson, to whom I have already gratefully referred, used to say that *any* recognition of God's activity is through a response in faith—which is not blind credulity but a going-beyond the ready deliverance of human observation and human thinking. Thus when I say that God acts in nature and history, above all when I see an "act of God" in the event of Jesus Christ, I am not pointing to an *obvious* fact which anybody can recognize. I am saying that the "importance" of this or that occurrence, and notably of Jesus Christ, has awakened a responsive possibility in us. We may, or we may not, make this our own and think and act upon it. But if we do, it is perfectly proper to use as our symbolic expression words drawn from human experience such as I have employed.

In any event, in a conceptuality in which we have to do not with sheer *things* or with "presences" felt by us subjectively, but with foci of energy, fields of activity and happenings in nature and history, it is essential that we grasp the fact that our world is patient of, open to, and the sphere in which the supreme reality of Love-in-act is at work. As Sally McFague has said in her *Metaphorical Theology* (SCM Press, 1983), our only way of talking—if we are not to remain utterly silent about God—is precisely by the use of such metaphorical (if you will, parabolic and symbolic) kinds of language. Thus I have no hesitation in saying that "God acts," although I am quite sure that I must say it with due recognition of its inadequacy and limitations.

What is affirmed in Christian faith and enacted in Christian worship is expressed in Christian living, as men and women realize in themselves and manifest in their behavior the same reality of Love-in-act. Thus they become what some have been prepared to call "other Christs." Both St. Benedict and Martin Luther thus spoke of every Christian as *alter Christus,* one in whom and by whom the divine Love is at work to establish the sovereignty of that divine Love in the creation by overcoming hatred, oppression, injustice, and all manner of evil. The ultimate purpose is that God "shall be all and in all," which is to say that cosmic Love-in-act shall be shown victorious over whatever has opposed or threatened it. In the divine life itself this victory is accomplished. In the created order, whether this one that we now know or some other about which we can know nothing, this victory is also to be accomplished, not by imposition from on high but by the "co-creating" activity of God and the creatures who (as I have urged) possess both creaturely dignity and creaturely responsibility.

What has been written so far in this chapter may seem to some a long and perhaps tedious exposition; but it was necessary if what follows is to make sense to the reader. More will be said about it in the later chapters of this book. It provides, as I have said, an invaluable setting for, as well as an approach to, a consideration of how we today may most satisfactorily describe our human condition with its evident "wrongness." It also provides a setting for and an approach to a contemporary grasp of what in Christian faith we affirm to be God's deliverance of men and women from their "wrongness," setting them on the right path and enabling them to live as sons and daughters of the God from whose love they have come and to whose love they are intended to go as their final destiny.

First, then, what is "wrong" about us men and women, as we today understand ourselves and would describe our condition? I think that we must say something like what follows, which I can conveniently style a kind of word-picture. Of course there are many who will not readily accept this picture. They will say that they are not at all troubled and that they do not feel there is anything particularly "wrong" with them, or at least nothing which more opportunity, better income, easier living conditions, and the like will not remove. Yet

I suspect that even such men and women, who to my mind seem to be living a somewhat superficial life, have their moments of what Henry David Thoreau once called "quiet desperation"—when they cannot sleep, perhaps, or when for a few moments life seems to "get them down."

But I must complete the sketch of my word-picture. From time to time large numbers, if not all, of our contemporaries have a feeling of meaninglessness in their lives. They have a sense of dissatisfaction with things around them and on occasion are unhappy with themselves. What is behind that feeling and sense? Tillich put it well, I think, when he spoke of an inability to accept oneself as one is and for what one is, with an honest recognition of one's good and bad points. "I am not what I ought to be and what I could be," they might say if pressed very hard. Because of this inability to accept oneself and to acknowledge that one is not, or not yet, realizing a fully harmonious and rounded human life, there is great difficulty in accepting other people as *they* are and for what *they* are. Many modern novels, not to mention much contemporary poetry and drama, tell us about this. There is more to be said, however, and here Abelard's insight is significant. Basically, it seems to me that this inability to accept self and to accept others rests back upon an even deeper feeling and sense. I refer here to the "levelessness" which marks the lives of so many people today. It is not only that they find it difficult if not impossible *to love*—and I am not talking here about their capacity for and enjoyment of sexual experience, which is related to but not identical with the ability to love. They also find it very hard *to be loved*, with the demands that "being loved" make upon them.

Deep and true love, so much desired and so infrequently achieved, is essentially a matter of giving-and-receiving. It is a mutual relationship. It is a matter of mutual commitment and trust, with hopefulness for the best in others. It is a readiness to make sacrifices, so that those who are loved may be better and happier persons. What is more, it requires a certain "death" to self when this self is taken to be for self's sake alone. William Blake was right in saying that every act of genuine kindness is a "little death to self." Every experience of human separation from another is also a "dying of self" because the other has somehow become identified with oneself. Those who

have been in the position of serving as advisor or counselor for other
people know that those who ask for such advice and counsel are almost
always in need of love, want to love, and need and want *to be* loved;
they have discovered that this is so difficult, so often a failure, that
they despair of themselves—which, of course, is why they turn to
somebody who they hope may be able to help them.

Levelessness also means loneliness. If we look at the world
today we are struck by the amount of sheer loneliness there is about
us. "The lonely crowd" was the title of a book published some years
ago; its author pointed out that few people are so lonely, and feel
so much isolated and separated from others, as those who are constantly *with* others in terms of physical propinquity. I have often
observed the faces of men and women, even quite young people,
on the London underground and the New York subway system. Eliot's
words about such people, "distracted by distraction from distraction,"
have seemed to me to speak accurately. But even more obvious is
the withdrawal into self and the appearance of near depression which
can be noticed—not all the time, to be sure, but plainly visible again
and again.

Unacceptability, levelessness, loneliness—and along with these
there is a disturbing feeling that nothing much can be done about
it. Hence there is the sense of impotence to handle life, to meet it
head-on, and to achieve some measure of genuine human harmony
and contentment.

Now if this is anything like an accurate word-picture of the
condition of vast numbers of men and women today, as I am sure
it is, then it is to people in just this condition that the Christian message
of deliverance is to be addressed. But before I turn to that promise
of deliverance, I must first say something about what to some readers
will have seemed a strange silence in the discussion so far. "What
about sin?" they may ask. "You have not mentioned *that;* and surely
for the Christian tradition as it has come down to us the basic problem
in men and women is their sinfulness, both as a condition and as
concrete acts." To this my answer is that, in fact, I have been talking
about sinfulness all along. To be sure, I have not spoken of it in the
conventional ways; and this I freely acknowledge because I think that
the conventional presentation does not cut much ice or have much

meaning for the multitudes of people about whom I have been speaking. Let me say a few words about this difficult question. What is sin? What are sins? The question of sinfulness must be reduced to these two different problems. *Sin* (in the singular) is the state or situation of men and women who find themselves in precisely the alienated and estranged condition (from self, from others, eventually from God) which I have been describing. Through millennia of human history and in consequence of untold numbers of personal decisions made during those ages, we have all of us been brought up in, and we now exist in, a human condition in which we know (sometimes vividly, sometimes vaguely) that we are unacceptable, loveless, lonely and impotent. "We have no power of ourselves to help ourselves." The millions of wrong choices, alien to or against proper and fulfilling human development towards living in love, acceptance and relationship, have brought this about. And our *sins* (in the plural) are the inumerable and various words, deeds, thoughts, gestures and other outward or internal expressions in which we make specific wrong choices, about ourselves and about others and ultimately *coram dei* or before God. It is not so much that in an obvious fashion we are blasphemous, impious or irreverent. Rather, it is that we are unconcerned, careless, indifferent, unloving, not ready to take risks for others who are in "a bad way," not bothered about the appalling injustice and oppression in the world, lacking serious regard for the common lot and failing to grasp the opportunity to contribute to human amelioration. So sin and sins are very much in this word-picture, once we have understood them in a sense more profound and searching than the easy, glib and altogether too "religious" way of speaking about them which has become conventional in religious circles.

To be sure, ultimately all sin is *against God*. But then we must be clear about the meaning of that little word "God." For the central Christian tradition God is worshipful, supreme, dependable, and above all loving; indeed God *is* love, Love-in-act, known to humans who exist in the world. Yet God is active and hence present in the creation in whatever is good, true, just, honorable, lovely, enriching, fulfilling, demanding of caring action and responsive. This activity is under many different incognitos and with many different "names." To that point we shall turn in a later note. Whatever impedes or denies or rejects or minimizes or refuses invitations, lures, solicitations, attractions and demands of caring in these most various areas of life is thus to be seen as having the nature of sin. For sin is a "backwater existence," without movement forward as part of the creative advance; it is found in the falsely self-centered, self-regarding, other-neglecting and other-rejecting acts and thoughts and words to which we humans are prone and for which we are accountable. God is in no sense responsible here; these are the consequences of decisions in a creation in which there is freedom and responsibility for all the created agents. To paraphrase a remark of Whitehead's, all these wrong things matter and they all have consequences which must be faced honestly and openly. But God is in this struggle. He is the chief agency in the world process of "amorization" or "love-making"; and as he shares in this enterprise so also he is actually at work in it as the "fellow sufferer who understands," again in Whitehead's words. The divine victory is to be seen in that context; so also the divine glory is in dedicated love-sharing rather than in supernatural splendor, pomp and regality.

The Christian gospel, whose historical grounding is in the apostolic witness to the event of Jesus Christ, has at its heart the proclamation that this God who is Love-in-act has not only been disclosed through and has shared in the experience of God's children at all times and in all places. God has also taken action in that event (in what for Christians is a decisive and focal fashion), with the intention to deliver them from what they and he know to be "wrong" about their lives and from what hinders their becoming, along with all their fellow-humans, persons who are moving "towards the image of God." That is, God seeks to actualize, to the fullest degree possible for humans, their God-derived potentiality to become created, finite and (since they *are* finite and mortal) defective lovers, whose existence will be in a relationship of give-and-take, of accepting and being accepted. Thus God delivers them also from terrifying loneliness; and God strengthens them with might by the Spirit in their inward being. They may become "more than conquerors through him who loved" them. Their destiny, if they continue in this grace released for them in that event of Jesus Christ, is a reception by God into the divine life. Here is an enriching of God (and I dare to say this, despite a long tradition which denies God any such possibility since he is thought already and always to "have it all made") as they are treasured by God and open to God's employment. In this world with its particular style (or in some other world of God's creating with *its* particular style of existence) they provide God with "material" for further activity in love.

Now the questions must be asked: *how* does such deliverance take place, once we have granted the situation and conditions and circumstances which we see to be ours today? How can our human "wrongness" be set right? How can we be brought into "newness of life" and given the ability to continue in that newness when we exist as we do in a world which is imperfect and which contains so much that is evil and unjust and false and unlovely? This is the question, or the set of questions, to which I shall devote much of the remainder of this and the next chapter, in the hope that something may be said which will be helpful and meaningful. We need always to remember that our current awareness of the human position is not identical with that of our fathers and mothers in the faith, although we can and must be ready to learn from them as in their own fashion they faced and understood their "wrongness."

The first point for us to note is that there is a two-way movement here. It is a movement between God and humankind; it is also between humankind and God. The Process conceptuality is a special help to us at this point because it makes it possible for us better to understand this double movement: *from God* who is the primal creative cause and the source of the lures which invite response from those to whom they come; and *from the human side*, with the response of men and women who accept the lures and seek to adopt as their "subjective aim" or purpose in life both the "initial aim" given in their very existence and the continuing invitations they receive from God to actualize their human possibility. God affects and influences his or her human children. In their turn they answer him or her in that what they become and do makes a contribution to the divine life. In biblical thought and in Christian experience this kind of divine-human duality is to be seen everywhere. On the one hand there is grace, which is God's love actively directed towards us; on the other hand there is faith, which is commitment and a loyal "amen" made

2-part process

to God by the humans to whom such grace has come. In one way
or another, all Christian thought has stressed both sides.

In the second place, there is a subjective and objective aspect
in what is going on in human deliverance. On the latter, or objective,
side, God is *doing* something. God really *is* at work in the world. God
does act in the event of Christ, revealing the divine nature and intention
for humankind, while at the same time releasing through that event
the power to love of which humankind stands in so much need if
there is indeed to be a genuine participation for men and women
in the divine purpose. On the former or subjective side, there is the
human awareness of and the human answer to what is being disclosed
and released. Revelation is not revelation at all, unless there is
somebody who receives it; without reception it is ineffectual. Alter-
natively, unless there is something really done, something truly given,
there is no point or significance in human aspiration. Years ago William
Temple remarked that in the Christian picture there is a "coincidence,"
as he called it, "divine initiative" and "human apprehension" or
discernment. We may extend this by saying that just such objective-
subjective situations are a reality everywhere. There is the objective
fact: the artist paints a picture, the novelist writes a book, the poet
produces a piece of verse, or the actors present a drama. But unless
somebody sees the picture, reads the novel, grasps the message which
the poem seeks to communicate, or appreciates and values the actors'
characterizations—unless there is this subjective side the whole
enterprise comes to nothing at all. Above all, we see this duality in
the human experience of love; for love is always a two-way activity,
with those who are "in love" mutually involved both in the loving
and in the being loved. There is objectivity about the situation, in
that there is the fact of this or that lover acting lovingly; and there
is also subjectivity, seen in the beloved's saying, usually through act
rather than word, that he or she accepts such loving, delights in it,
and finds enrichment from it.

Thus we might say that to humans in their *need* of love God comes
with his *deed* of love. To put it in that fashion, however, is to talk
in quite general terms true enough to be sure, but lacking the vividness
and sharp appeal which a particular instance alone can provide. G. K.
Chesterton once said that the Lord "commanded us to love, not the

human race, but our fellow men and women." Love always personal-
izes; only by such personalization does it really "come across." We
must also remember that there is no such thing as an "individual"
man or woman. We are *persons*, which as St. Thomas Aquinas among
others pointed out long ago means that we are capable of relationships.
Indeed, the "topic" of religion, in Whitehead's phrasing, is the
"individual in community"—or as I should prefer to put it, "persons-
in-society." But this is the case in more than religion only. This is
the "topic" for *all* discourse which is concerned to stress the way
humans in fact do live—with others, from others, by others and for
others, either negatively to their hurt or positively to their fulfillment.
In the sort of language which Tillich used, we must insist that only
when we are mutually accepting and know ourselves somehow to
be acceptable can there be a genuine growth in human existence
towards making actual our common human possibility. So again, only
when there is love given *and* love received is there a chance for the
establishment of the sort of mutuality which enhances life and
guarantees justice among and between men and women. Here, of
course, the Abelardian insight comes to our aid.

There is still another consideration which should be stressed.
Humans are not static and fixed creatures; like everything else in
the creation they are on the move. It is absurd to think that we can
"stop" this movement at some convenient point. Human existence
is essentially a direction being followed or a route being taken. Our
human identity is found in our memory of the past, from which we
humans come; in our awareness of the present, where decisions (either
negative or positive) are taken; and in our movement towards a future,
of which anticipations (in the strict sense of that word, namely hints
or intimations or glimpses) are already being given. That is how we
men and women live. The question for us is whether the past (which
has provided the "stuff" for our "prehensions" or graspings), the present
(in which we are making our choices), and the goals (towards which
we aim), are for good or for bad, for diminishment of existence or
for enhancement of it. This might be phrased more accurately by
saying that while such is indeed our human situation, it is *we ourselves*
who determine whether and how we answer it, by acting either for
that which is good or for that which is bad. Our human tragedy is

that because of the millennia of wrong decisions, which in our sociality inevitably affect and influence us, and also because of our own decisions, we fail both as persons and in our social life to move towards fulfillment. Our sense of unacceptability and our incapacity genuinely to love, the self-immersion which makes us lonely people, along with the lack of power to change by our own effort alone, combine to present us with what certainly seems a dark and gloomy picture.

Yet, as I said, the Christian proclamation is that to us in our need of love and acceptance, God comes—decisively in the event of Jesus Christ for us in our Christian tradition although doubtless in other ways and through other agencies for non-Christians. God comes with his deed of love and acceptance; that is what the gospel is about. That is what the social process that is the Church's living tradition is commissioned to proclaim and to enact in the affairs of the world. Therefore the questions which are put to every son and daughter of God are these: Will you commit yourself, with all the risk involved, to prevenient divine Love-in-act? Will you make this Love-in-act the center of your human existence? Will you open yourself to receive and to respond to this Love-in-act? Will you let yourself be used, as a person-in-social-relationships, so that this Love-in-act may be available to others through your caring for them, through your devotion to their best growth, and through your readiness to work for their release from whatever oppresses them and denies them their dignity as men and women? In other words, Will you let this Love-in-act master you, nourish you and strengthen you? To the last question, which sums up all the others, we may answer with a "Yes" or with a "No." Nobody, and plainly not God, who is Love, can coerce us. The response must be our own and nobody's else.

I have urged elsewhere that one of the difficulties with what has come to be taken as orthodox theology is the use of certain "models" for God and for God's relationship with the creation, which produce a view that is far removed from our concrete human experience. The tendency has been to think of deity in terms of immutable, impassable, and unrelated "being itself"; or in terms of a ruler who is entirely in control of everything in the creation; or in terms of a "ruthless moralist" who punishes or rewards men and women for obeying or disobeying rules laid down arbitrarily by that moralist. Whitehead characterized these models as nothing but "idols," and he considered that the Christian Church, in accepting them, has been guilty of serious apostasy from what he splendidly called the "brief Galilean vision" of God as Love—not impotent and ineffectual love, to be sure, but love with its demand *and* its graciousness. When such false "models" are accepted, the understanding of the relationship sustained between God and the creation is bound to reflect them. Many of the conventional interpretations of redemption have been in line with these views of God and God's ways in the world. But surely the only approach which is possible for those who take with utmost seriousness the witness of the apostolic tradition is one in which the analogies, or perhaps better the symbols, which we employ are drawn from what we know so well in our human personal-social existence.

Obviously God is not *just like* the relationships which we have with one another in our common life, even at its best. The divine mystery cannot be violated; and in everything said about God and God's doings, there is always an *O altitudo*, as Sir Thomas Browne says in *Religio Medici*. Whatever symbols we use; whatever principles we find necessary to explain our human experience so far as we are able; whatever language we employ when talking about God and ourselves; these can only be suggestive and their application to God must always be in an *eminent* fashion, to use the idiom of scholastic thought. Nonetheless, this is where we *must* start, for it is the only place from which humans can start; only in this area do we have genuine knowledge. Hence I insist that we should look at our own awareness of human relationships for a clue to *divine-human* relationships. That is the procedure which I have sought to follow in the preceding discussion. I am convinced that it makes sense of God's deliverance of us and "setting right" what is "wrong" about us. Furthermore, I am convinced that it can be meaningful to men and women in our own day, as other and earlier interpretations are not.

It is possible for us to demythologize the early biblical talk about demon-possession and God's victory over Satan and his minions. It is also possible to see the point in what was said about freedom from slavery, about acquittal from juridical sentence of condemnation, and even about belief in God's providing for men and women sufficient "penitence" and a capacity rightly to honor the divine majesty, as well as about the gift of new life. We can grasp this last conception ("newness of life") most readily when talk of "corruption and mortality" is supplanted by talk of life-in-love as overcoming life-without-love. In all these ancient pieces of interpretation there had been a discernment of the enduring truth that God has done something for us which we desperately needed to have done. And talk about following Jesus' reported teaching also has its point, since the significance of what Jesus *said*, or is reported to have said, is primarily found in its indicating the kind of impression he made upon those who told stories about his concrete existence in Palestine and hence under what circumstances deliverance was wrought. Yet none of this requires us to accept literally those ways of understanding such deliverance, which as Christians we affirm has in very fact taken place.

One issue remains, however. In what sense can we maintain what used to be called the "finality" of Christ and of this Christian deliverance, without succumbing to the attitude which Arnold Toynbee used to call "Christian imperialism"? In our "global village," where we have learned so much about cultures and religions other than the ones readily familiar to us, is it still possible to speak meaningfully of the *decisive nature* of the event of Jesus Christ—a phrase which surely is a more satisfactory expression for what used to be styled "finality." To this issue we now address ourselves.

I have spoken earlier of the originating event for Christianity as the "*classical* instance" (I now italicize the adjective because of its importance). To speak of a classical instance is to contradict the conventional notion that what happened in the event of Jesus Christ was what I have sometimes phrased a "supreme anomaly." This latter phrase would suggest that the event is unique, with no parallels in, no approximations to, no associations with, and no resemblances to what goes on elsewhere. Rudolf Bultmann seems to have spoken in this mistaken fashion, unless I have entirely misunderstood his argument; and he has been criticized by Karl Jaspers and by Fritz Buri, the Swiss philosophical theologians, and by Schubert Ogden and others in English-speaking theology, for precisely this error.

But the special value in speaking of a "classical instance," as contrasted with what I just styled a "supreme anomaly" is that it illustrates and exemplifies in a decisive fashion what is going on in a wider way. Earlier I made this point when I urged that what otherwise might be a vaguely perceived and barely grasped truth must have a vivid meaning which we are able in some degree to understand. A classical instance gives a cutting-edge to the more general truth which is in view. Often, if not always, it is the occasion for our new or renewed awareness of that more general truth, which otherwise might not be seen for what it is. Furthermore, it can have the effect of releasing for those to whom it comes a capacity to see themselves differently and hence to modify their own pattern of life and behavior.

Just here we begin to understand that what Ogden has spoken about under the heading of "the point of Christology" has its importance and its relevance. In that classical instance we can discern in a decisive and hence especially effectual fashion what God is always and everywhere doing in the world. But even more valuable for us, we can learn the truth about every human existence at any time since humankind became what now we know it to be. Each of us is responsible, capable of choice with ability to act more or less in accordance with decisions made; each of us has been given a dignity and value; and our significance is precisely that each of us can be open to the working of God's love. The end-product can be an existence which is "in love" and which moves towards fulfillment in and under God, who *is* Love-in-act. In other words, we know from the decisive or classical instance that there is in every human life a possibility of such loving as the meaning of every genuinely human existence. We can also discern that there have been and are various realizations or other actualizations of that possibility which have no obvious connection with the decisive act of God found in Jesus himself in its own specificity; yet that these can be properly interpreted in the light of that same act.

In the ancient Church the so-called Fathers of Christian theology had their own, and of course very different, way of grasping this point and speaking about it. For some of them the *Logos spermatikos,* or seminal word, was said to be present in every human life; for them it pointed towards the *Logos sarkotheis* or the full "enmanment" of that Logos or Word in Jesus Christ. There was talk by St. Athanasius about the relationship between the Word "by whom all things were made" and the same Word "incarnate" in Jesus Christ, a relationship which permitted Athanasius to speak of creation at large *and* of Jesus Christ in particular as both of them *organons*, or instrumental agencies, for God's revealing and redeeming activity. Later on in the Middle Ages, there was the Thomist insistence that God's grace is everywhere present, not least in all sound human rational endeavor. There has also been a further development of the primitive idea that baptism, as entrance into the community which was regarded as the carrier of salvation, could be by "martyrdom" (when the actual rite for some reason could not be performed but there was witness to Christ to the point of death) or by "desire" (when a man or woman or child wished to be received into the Church but was for some reason prevented from actually being baptized). In some recent philosophers and theologians (notably by Jacques Maritain in our own time and by Baron vonHügel before him) there has been the affirmation that any man or woman who has responded to as much of the truth as was available to him or her could be considered as "saved." There have been several other ways of making the same point. The Second Vatican Council, for example, had much to say about good faith as response to whatever was known about God in non-Christian circumstances and about the possibility of life lived with dignity and responsibility under other faiths and in other religious traditions.

This more generous attitude has been neglected only by men like Tertullian in the ancient Church, the Jansenists in the post-Reformation Catholic Church, narrowly biblicist evangelicals in more recent times, and some Lutherans who have a spoken (like Bultmann, as I understand him) of absolute uniqueness and utter necessity for faith in the specific historical figure of Jesus Christ. These have denied what is known technically in post-Reformation circles as the *extra Calvinisticum* (Calvin's teaching that God is known and served by many apart from—*extra*—that specific act in Jesus Christ). Biblical texts have often been cited to support this exclusivist position. The texts chosen say much about its being "only" in Jesus that there is salvation. And of course there are Jesus' own reported sayings in which we hear about "the few" who shall enter into God's kingdom.

In response to this narrowing of salvation or deliverance, Schubert Ogden (the theologian whom I have already cited several times) has made some pointed comments. One of them is this: "The claim 'only in Jesus Christ' must be interpreted to mean, not that God acts to redeem only in the history of Jesus and in no other history, but that the only God who redeems any history—*although he in fact redeems every history*—is the God whose redemptive action is decisively represented in the word that Jesus speaks and is" (*The Reality of God*, p. 172, italics in the original.) Again and in that same book (p. 185-6) Ogden writes "To say with the Christian community . . . that Jesus is the decisive act of God is to say that in him, in his outer acts of symbolic word and deed, there is expressed that understanding of human existence which is, in fact, the ultimate truth about our life before God; that the ultimate reality with which we and all men have to do is God the sovereign Creator and Redeemer; and that in understanding ourselves in terms of the gift and demand of love, we realize our authentic existence as men."

This last quotation brings us to another and related issue. If we dare not be guilty of "Christian imperialism" by presenting the event of Jesus Christ as the exclusive and solitary divine act of deliverance, what can be said about Christian "mission" with its concern to proclaim Jesus Christ to non-Christians? About this matter I have two or three suggestions.

In the first place, the point of such a mission is not to "save from hell" the millions who have never heard about Jesus Christ. Certainly at some times and by some persons this has been taken to be the meaning of Christian mission. But who could claim that it is *we* who by our proclamation bring deliverance to anybody? *God* is the final judge of men and women. And if Christian faith is correct, God is sheer Love-in-act—God's generosity, as well as God's demand, is not limited and partial, like our own. Can we then conceive, even as the most remote possibility, that the "God and Father of our Lord Jesus Christ" would condemn to damnation the untold numbers of men and women who, before Jesus' time or after his time or wherever they may be and whenever they may have lived, have not heard of Jesus Christ, through no fault of their own; or who, for some reason, have found themselves unable to "accept him as Savior"? Traditional Christian teaching about "invincible ignorance," either by lack of opportunity or by an inherent inability to grasp and accept Jesus Christ for whatever reason, has been "devised," so to say, by Catholic

Christianity as a way of "handling" these people and treating them fairly and honestly.

But, in the second place, responsibility is still laid upon those who have known deliverance specifically through Jesus Christ to share this knowledge with others. Precisely because through response to him they themselves have found "newness of life" and "joy and peace in believing," they are impelled to this sharing. But that can be done without assuming that apart from it those others are "without hope." In his letter to the Romans St. Paul writes about his wish to share with them "some spiritual gift." Anybody whose existence has been made new through Christ must also want to "share a spiritual gift." If he or she does not desire this, we can only conclude that such a person has not really been "converted" in heart and soul and mind, but only in a superficial and undemanding fashion, to the significance of the originative Christian event.

Third, we who are within the Christian tradition and are participants in the social process whose originating moment was in the event to which the apostolic witness was borne, know a life within that ongoing tradition which is marked by a concern that requires an invitation to others to "join" and participate in the love that is there available. Hence our responsibility is not to "rescue souls from the burning," one by one as individuals; it is to bring as many as will respond into a fellowship, to share a common life which has known the decisive disclosure in Christ and has been "engraced," by the release in that place of God's love, to live "in love and charity" with others.

In recent years some few wise theologians have been prepared to say even more. They have argued that precisely because God has left nobody "without witness" to the possibility of life with God and the understanding of human existence as nothing other than the opportunity to respond to God in love and obedience and hence to realize what is potentially theirs as men and women, the several non-Christian religious movements (and also such non-religious positions as genuinely promote fullness of life) are themselves to be seen as channels or avenues which God delights to use. Furthermore, they urge that God has been in them and has been their ultimate source. The Roman Catholic theologian Paul Knitter (of Xavier University in the United States) has written admirably along these lines in a series of essays in *Concilium* and elsewhere. The practical conclusion here is that there is need for dialogue with non-Christians, whether they are participant in some other religious tradition or are without any conscious religious convictions, including even those who would call themselves "atheists." What have such people to teach us? And what have we to teach them? Those of us who are within the living tradition of Christian faith, worship and obedience surely have something to teach and something to learn from those who are not in this position.

We serve the truth most adequately—although as created, finite, mortal and defective humans never completely or fully—when we adopt this generous or (as vonHügel said) "hospitable" attitude and way of acting. We can adopt this approach without for a moment negating the decisive quality *for us* of our own allegiance to the tradition to which we belong and to the Lord who is adored in that tradition. "When you and I wake up in Hell," I once naughtily put it in a sermon, "we may be surprised to see who is *not* there." We are in no position to judge other persons or to require God to behave in a fashion that to us seems to be "correct." Rather, we are in the position of men and women who have been drawn to respond to God's focal act in Jesus Christ and who are learning, painfully yet rewardingly, to live in and under the divine Love there available. We are those who must endeavor to bring the whole of the *orbis terrarum* to know that same Love in whatever fashion may be possible for them. We are in the position of those who realize the demand laid upon them to do "the works of love" by bringing to others release from oppression and by seeking to be agents for God's sovereignty in love in every aspect of human affairs. Otherwise we are only "unprofitable servants."

4

A Note on God's Secular Incognitos

In discussing God's working in nature, history and human experience, in ways that are not, so to say, "tagged" with the divine name, I shall venture to write personally. Only so, in my judgment, can I manage to communicate a conviction that has grown in me over the years; and which I believe to be very relevant to the subject of this book.

It is my privilege and delight to be a member of King's College in Cambridge, a place which every year is visited by thousands of tourists. Its chapel—surely one of the most magnificent buildings in the world with a deserved reputation for the splendor of its music—is an attraction for vast multitude of people from every land. They come in astonishing numbers to attend the services in chapel: the other day I think there were about eight hundred at a Sunday Evensong. As one who is regularly present at the daily services and who is given the opportunity to assist in them and often preach at them, I am continually struck by the response which these visitors make to what goes on within the chapel.

Often enough, as one stands at the back of the chapel after a service, one is told by visitors how much they have appreciated the worship and how greatly they have been moved by our way of doing it. What is more important, they are likely to say (although often in their own idiom, which may not be at all conventionally "pious") that they have "experienced" what they sometimes call "a sense of something more than human" or "a feeling of being caught up into heaven" or "to have been taken out of this world." They may use some other similar and perhaps not always too happy a way of letting one know that for them it has not been so much a fine musical "performance" as a genuine act of worship through which they have come to a realization of the "transcendent."

I begin this note in this way because I have *also* been told, by clergymen and others, that "people go to King's only because of the music and not to worship God." One young college chaplain in Cambridge refused to come to any of our services because (as he once said to me) "it's nothing but a concert." All this has made me think seriously about the question, Does God make himself known to us time and again in nonreligious ways and through secular incognitos? To this question my own unhesitating answer is "Yes." In this chapter I propose to say something about the richness and variety of the divine action and hence the divine self-disclosure, made so frequently in ways that are not immediately and directly "religious."

The late J. B. Phillips once wrote a book whose title was *Your God is Too Small*. I have forgotten what he said in the book; but the title seemed and still seems to me to be extraordinarily suggestive. Indeed, I used that very title in responding to one of those who spoke critically of worship at King's. When he said that "most people here today have come just for the music and the beauty of the place and they have no 'religious' motivation whatsoever," I replied (I hope not too sharply) "I think that your God is too small." He was astonished and annoyed, evidently not having any idea of the point which I was trying to make. This chapter, therefore, is my attempt to make precisely that point: that the God with whom we are or ought to be concerned is much bigger, much more all-embracing, and much more generous in relating himself or herself to humans than we often recognize. And in the second place, we need to enlarge our picture of God so that it will include within it the divine presence and the divine activity *in everything* that is good and right and true, in everything that evokes love, in everything that requires us to seek justice, and in everything that enriches and fulfills human aspiration and human longing.

First of all, then, I urge that in the historic Christian tradition, God is not taken to be concerned only with a privileged minority who happen to be what may be styled "religiously minded," who conform to some prescribed set of beliefs, or who belong to some particular religious group of society. George Tyrrell, the tragic Roman Catholic Modernist of the early part of this century, once said, "The word 'catholic' is music to my ears; for it makes me think of him whose arms were spread wide on the cross, not for a select few but for the whole of the *orbis terrarum*." Anything that would "narrow or canalize"—to use a phrase from Tyrrell's friend Baron vonHügel—this wide catholicity has been rejected and condemned by that age-long living tradition. This is often forgotten by those who in their praiseworthy devotion to their specific Christian conviction are prepared to deny or at least ready to call into question the significance of nonreligious approaches to the mystery by which we are surrounded and in which our little human lives are set. Faber's somewhat sentimental hymn speaks of "the wideness of God's mercy"; we shall do well to remember this divine "wideness" and refuse to confine the action of God to religious places and religious positions which for us have been highly important and rewarding.

If this more generous understanding of divine presence and action is accepted, it will follow that we should not seek to force God into some humanly devised straitjacket, nor should we try always to tag any given enriching experience or profound expression of care and concern with the divine name. In other words, we should be prepared to see (with St. Augustine, incidently) that God has many names. In his *Confessions* Augustine called God *veritas* (truth) and *pulchritudo* (beauty) and on occasion used other and similar words which to him seemed appropriate to the cosmic reach of deity.

In an earlier writing of mine, I ventured to report an experience of my own that made this point vividly clear to me. I had been at a superb rendition of Brahms's Fourth Symphony by the Boston Symphony Orchestra under Serge Koussevitzky. I had been deeply moved; and especially during the *passacaglia* in the fourth movement I had felt taken out of myself so entirely that it seemed that I was no longer in the concert-hall but in heaven itself. The next morning it occurred to me that during this concert I had been as close as I had ever come to having a "religious experience." Why then, I asked myself, had I not at once recognized it as such? But as soon as I asked myself this question, I was obliged to answer that it was much better that I had delighted in the music in all its own integrity and beauty and that I had responded to it precisely in its own fashion of speaking to the auditor. It would have been almost blasphemous, I saw, for me to try to make that evening's joy and sadness—for they go together in Brahms' Fourth—a specifically "religious" affair. It had been much better, indeed it had been entirely right and proper, for me to adore God in that secular incognito of musical splendor. It was afterward, in the recollection of the emotion, that I could and should and did know that the deep truth was that *God,* the transcendent yet immanent reality that is worshipful, dependable and unsurpassable, had been speaking to me and acting upon me that evening.

I apologize for relating this highly personal story, but I am sure that it helps to make the point with which I am concerned in this chapter. We need always to respect the divine "incognito," to accept it as it is and for what it does; only then, in the "recollection in tranquillity" which comes after the fact, may we come to grasp the truth that *God* has been there and has moved us to respond in an appropriate fashion.

This principle can be extended to include *all* the ways in which men and women are moved, influenced, attracted and lured to see truth, delight in beauty, seek after justice and respond in love precisely through their experience of that which is greater than themselves, more exigent and more gracious, inescapably present and unmistakably enriching and demanding. When the great American Quaker John Woollman felt obligated to labor for the enslaved blacks in the American colonies and thereafter in the new American republic, he spoke of "something laid upon his heart" which required just this devoted response in action. Similarly, with another American, Eugene V. Debs, the famous socialist leader in the first part of this century, who went to prison saying that "so long as one person is unjustly jailed" he was obliged to feel that *he* was in prison. The consequence was his zealous dedication to the struggle for social and economic justice in his own day. In so doing, he was a witness to the nonreligious but profoundly demanding voice of God within him. All these are liberating moments when humans find themselves freed from self-interest and given purpose in life.

The same sort of thing may be noted in the realm of scientific

research, observation and experiment. Many of my close friends in
New York, while I was teaching there, and now many more in
Cambridge, are scientists of great distinction. I frequently observe
their "humility before the fact," as Thomas Huxley once said about
Charles Darwin; I admire their dedication to their task, their deep
concern for truth and their sacrificial giving of themselves to their
work. Most of them, I suppose, would not easily speak about God
at all; certainly they would not usually talk in a "religious" idiom. Yet
I am convinced that in the scientific enterprise which is theirs they
are serving the only God there is, the God who *is* "truth," however
unwilling or unable they may be to give a name to what they know
so well and reverence so completely.

Another instance of the same truth which has often been in my
mind is the simple, unrewarded, yet totally committed fashion in which
parents care for their children, sacrificing themselves so that those
children may have a rich and fulfilling life. So also is response to the
call of duty and a readiness to give oneself to causes that are worth-
while and important. Nobody would wish to say that these are
"religious" in a narrow sense. Yet surely a believer in God must
recognize that these are places where that God is at work.

For me personally music is the way in which I most readily discern
this divine "incognito." But for others there will be different yet equally
compelling avenues or channels. Our conception of the divine working
in the world should be big enough to include all of them. Indeed
we might well take such a hymn as the one addressed to the Holy
Spirit, which speaks of the gifts of "coolness in the heat," "rest after
toil," "fire that lightens and burns," "gracious acceptance," and the
like, and turn the verses around so that we are prepared to say that
wherever, whenever and however such coolness, rest, fire and
acceptance are found, *there* God is most certainly present. Or again,
in the great words of the old Roman Catholic Holy Week liturgy,
ubi caritas et amor, ibi deus est—"where love and self-giving are present,
there God is." To recognize this charity and self-giving, and then to
respond to it, does not require that we should always be able to give
it the proper name.

If things are like that, what is the value and importance of our
Christian affirmation? What does our insistence, made in faith, that

in the event of Jesus Christ the divine Reality is both disclosed and released have to contribute? If the wider and more general revelation is so often known under such "secular" incognitos, why should there be a specific and (as traditional theology puts it) "special" revelation? The answer to this set of questions was suggested to me by a conversation with an acquaintance some years ago. We were talking about the disturbing fact that political power, as Lord Acton had said, seems almost inevitably to lead to corruption. My acquaintance remarked that while this was indeed a general truth, it needed particular "instances" (as he phrased it) and he spoke the name of one man in public life whose shocking career had brought home to us (and had given a cutting-edge to) this truth, and thus had made a difference in our attitudes. So it is, I should urge, that the Christian conviction that "God was in Christ," and that in Christ God "was reconciling us to himself," has its importance. Here is what earlier in this book I have styled the "*classical* instance," rather than the entirely unparalleled anomaly.

Because the event of Jesus Christ, witnessed in the living Christian tradition, is thus *classical* (and I italicize the adjective once more) it does two things. It discloses what God is always and everywhere "up to in the world." Also, and more vitally, it releases for us the capacity or power to grasp this reality and to live in terms of it. Precisely and exactly because we can see this in Christ, our understanding of *all* enriching, rewarding, demanding, appraising, humbling and shared moments of illumination receives a vivid coloring and a renewed strength. That makes a difference, yet with no denial or rejection of God's many and more "anonymous" ways of working in the world and with us who are God's human children.

There is of course a danger in what I have been arguing up to this point. It is the danger of overlooking, minimizing, or at worst even denying the presence and reality of wrong, evil, distortion and ugliness, all of them so horribly present in the world. I am conscious of this peril and I should not wish to be seen as a cheerful, easily tolerant, and uncritical defender of a world where everything is thought to be for the best and where there is no risk of error and no possibility of sin. Anybody who can still subscribe to that kind of "liberalism" is either stupid or blind. At best, ours is a tragic world; and human

experience within it is also tragic, frustrated and limited. It is marked
by much sheer wickedness, much intentional wrong-doing and much
willful wrong-seeing.

It is just here, of course, that the specific instance—in the
Christian view of things, what I have styled the "classical instances"
of the event of Jesus Christ—provides a way of correction quite as
much as a way of completion. It is liberating; it frees us to see things
realistically. Furthermore, it enables us to recognize that whatever
is not congruous with that event's deep disclosure is *not* a working
of God but a defect or a distortion in the created order. I am not
here concerned with arguing, as elsewhere I should wish to do, that
God (once seen as Love-in-act humanly expressed in the Man Jesus
and in the consequences of his emergence in the realm of history-
nature) is never responsible for such defect and distortion. In an earlier
chapter 1 urged that "the limitation of God is his goodness," as was
said by my philosophical master Alfred North Whitehead. For me
this demands that I shall deny anything like *sheer* "omnipotence" to
God; and that I shall insist that God's effectual power, beyond keeping
the world a cosmos and not permitting it to become anarchic and
chaotic, is to be found in God's love and in God's loving. If this
suggests a limitation upon God, in that in at least one sense he is
not totally in control, so be it. There is nothing particularly Christian
(nor Jewish either) in requiring that deity shall be portrayed as all-
controlling power. Indeed, that view may very well be a serious form
of idolatry, like the popular conceptions of God as a moral tyrant,
a cosmic manipulator, or a despotic ruler. A Christian who knows
his business should have seen this. "Pure universal Love thou art,"
says a Wesley hymn which succinctly affirms the specific Christian
insight about God's nature and activity.

Thus I cannot subscribe to the now somewhat popular talk about
God's "dark side" and try to reconcile this dark side with God's also
being "pure unbounded Love." It is wiser to speak of the relative
freedom of the creatures, from the subatomic level up to conscious
human agency, and hence of their ability to make significant decisions
(with or without explicit awareness). In the light of such decisions
it is they who must be seen as responsible for results which often
enough are for ill rather than for good. In any event, there is no

guarantee that any and every human experience is necessarily and inevitably a response to what is objectively good, just, true, beautiful or right. In this chapter I am not saying anything like that. What I *am* saying is that in many different ways, under many different "incognitos," disguised in many garments, the divine reality is always operative in the world. I appeal again to the great Baron vonHugel in his generous acceptance of such variety and his readiness to honor and reverence those nonreligious disclosures and activities in which men and women have been given freedom through a glimpse of the "more"—the "more" which ultimately is nothing other than God as primal creative cause and final recipient of what is being accomplished for good in the world.

This is why I am glad when so many visitors to King's College Chapel tell me that they have had there some awareness of supreme beauty, some intimation of rich meaning, some hint of what I, if not they, would call the "transcendent-which-becomes-immanent" in all sorts of ways. Now and again such a visitor has said to me something like this: "I came to hear great music in a beautiful building, but I remained to worship God." That is good and right. But it would also be quite proper for someone to say that he or she had been profoundly affected by the splendid music and the glorious building, yet without feeling impelled to the "religious" naming of what it has meant. It is gratifying when someone does "remain to worship" consciously and knowingly, the God whom we who "do" the service seek to worship in our own chapel. But it is also good when the experience of great music in a beautiful setting evokes a response of delight and joy. For even then God *is* being worshiped, but under one of many incognitos. God *is* being given glory, even as God's human children are given some awareness of a great good. Above all, God is then acting to release men and women from false centering upon self and to free them to learn to live in love and in acceptance of life in its mystery.

5

The Place of the Cross

If the discussion which has preceded this chapter has value, a number of questions arise which require our attention: Why the Cross? What about justification and sanctification, commonly regarded in the Christian tradition as two "steps" in the redemptive movement? What about particular *sins*, if the human situation or condition in *sin* is what we have represented it to be? There are other questions which might be asked and some of them will be addressed in the succeeding chapters: What is the place of the Christian fellowship or "social process" in this context? What is the significance of the eucharist for the deliverance of humans from their wrongness? Is what has been said about redemption relevant to the contemporary concern known as "liberation theology." What is the role of prayer as part of Christian life?

First, why the Cross?

We must dismiss as superficial and irrelevant the so-called liberal notion that the crucifixion of Jesus Christ should be regarded merely as another tragic instance of human martyrdom, without any significant place in human deliverance. Of course there is a sense in which the death of Jesus is like other deaths in which persons who hold tenaciously to convictions they consider of the highest importance are prepared to die rather than deny those convictions. But the insight of the living Christian tradition has always been that there is something more than that in Jesus' passion and death, even if that tradition has also been prepared to claim that in their light the whole story of human martyrdom is given a heightened significance.

On the other hand, the belief that in some fashion the death of Jesus was part of God's predetermined will—and was included in the divine "foreknowledge" and central to God's initial "plan" for the world before ever humankind existed—seems to presuppose a picture of God which many of us find incredible. It is noteworthy that those who talk in these terms (as of course does much of the material in the New Testament itself) have usually taken biblical idiom as final and inerrant. Hence such theologians have tended to be on the strongly evangelical or biblicistic side. However, their view of deity is not possible for us if we take with utter seriousness the conviction that God is not to be seen as a dictatorial ruler possessed of the sort of omniscience which in one instant knows past, present and future. Nor do we see God as an immutable and impassible being who produces affects in the world but is not affected by what happens within it and to it. It is hard to reconcile this theology that portrays God as having designed a world in which the death of Jesus was part of some eternal plan to be a remedy for the wrongness which, in that same view, was also from all eternity equally a part of God's foreknowledge, with the belief that God's "nature and name" is nothing other than sheer love. Yet there may be a way in which the profound truth which these theologians express can be preserved without succumbing to what I can only consider sub-Christian concepts of the divine nature and purpose and activity.

The first step which must be taken when we consider the Cross requires a return to a point made in an earlier chapter. I urged that Abelard's contention that love is the clue to the meaning of Christ as the deliverer from human wrongness must be set in an ontological context. As it stands, this contention is indeed profoundly true and makes sense of the place of the event of Jesus Christ in Christian faith. But also, *as its stands* it lacks a backing in a wider picture of how things happen in the world at large. To be sure, it rules out once and for all the sub-Christian notion that God is a tyrant who demands satisfaction for the human wrongdoing that has offended the divine honor, just as it makes impossible any talk about God's nature as divided between justice and mercy. But it is not relevant in any talk

about the freeing of slaves, any more than it is with a theology which
speaks about God's supplying incorruption and immortality for
creatures who are caught in corruption and are necessarily mortal and
doomed to death. Its insistence is on God as so much the lover of
creatures that God is bound to act towards them in a fashion which
will both demonstrate to them and release for them the divine love.
That alone can make it possible for them to live in a responding love
towards God and a resultant love for their human brothers and sisters.
And Abelard is certainly right in affirming that a love like God's is
prepared to go to any lengths, even to the point of dying, so that
men and women can have abundance of life in love.

But what is lacking is a wider setting in which God and the world
are seen in such a relationship that not only does God *will* to act
in love, but that there is no other way in which God *can* act if the
deliverance of God's children is to be accomplished. Just here, I
believe, the Process conceptuality upon which I have laid such stress
comes to our aid. For in that conceptuality God is not seen as acting
upon the world, as it were "from outside." Rather, God is seen as acting
with and in the world and as genuinely affected by the world, because
the relationship between deity and the created order is such that only
by mutuality and participation can the divine purpose be realized.
In other words, God is so related to the world that God is effective
within it and affected by it.

On the one hand God does not stand remote from the world
nor on the other hand does God control it in its every detail. Thus
there is an openness and freedom in the created order; and with this
God must come to terms, with this God must act, and through this
God's ends must be accomplished. Otherwise, the creation, and above
all the human creation, stands to God like a robot to its manipulator
or as a puppet to its master. In a Process view, God is indeed all-
wise, since God knows all actuality and God knows all potentiality;
but God knows them exactly as they are: what is actual *as* actual and
what is possible *as* possible. Yet God does not dictate how things
shall turn out. God adapts the divine action to the exigencies of the
creation because God has full respect for its own integrity, its own
capacity to make decisions, and its own accountability for the
consequences which this entails.

What is more, the world is not a finished and completed affair; *it is being created.* There is no absolute predetermination about what takes place within it. Of course God knows possibilities and knows also that things can go wrong and that there is a certain inevitability about that wronggoing, granted creaturely freedom at all levels. God does not dictate this wrongdoing, however, either as a matter of direct will or as a matter of permissive will. God accommodates himself or herself to a creation which in its "creative advance" is responsible for decisions which are made in genuine creaturely freedom. Thus God's manner of working, like the divine nature in itself (and I have urged that in a profound sense the two are identical, since "a thing *is* what it *does*") is not by coercive control but by persuasive lure and appeal.

We can therefore come to see the death of Jesus Christ as being part of the total pattern of divine-human or divine-creature activity. It is not an isolated moment, entirely different from the way in which God is always both at work in and open to affects from the creation. Rather, as I have said earlier, it is the classical instance of the way things actually go with God and the world. The decisions of men and women have brought about a situation where they can and do reject good, despise justice, refuse loving, and hate the beautiful and true. This is a situation brought about not by a divine purpose that such rejections should occur, but by the willful, self-centered, unloving ways of human beings who are responsible and who must accept such responsibility. At the same time, however, God is deeply involved in it all, and participates as a fellow-sufferer who knows (from the inside, as it were) what all this means, and who shares in the anguish which it brings about.

The conventional view, which in its details I have rejected, has yet somehow discerned that in a world like ours it is inevitable that there shall be wrongdoing that results in a wrongful situation. It has also discerned that only by God's action can there be a deliverance from such a state of affairs. Where the view goes wrong, I urge, is in its picture of God and of God's relationship to creation. It has not been able to emancipate itself from pre-Christian and sub-Christian ideas of God and of God's ways of acting. It has not seen that God is sheer Love-in-act and that the world is both the object of this unfailing love and also the desired respondent to this love.

When the Cross is seen as integral to the very existence of the One who is at the heart of the Christian "event," and when it is also recognized as bringing to a climax the total self-giving which marked the whole existence of the Man of Nazareth (we recall here the medieval saying *tota vita Christi mysterium crucis*), there is a focus on God's action in the human existence of Jesus, just as there is also a focus on the wrongness of humankind in its continual rejection of lures, invitations, and appeals to respond in obedient love to the prior invitations of God.

Thus there is indeed an inevitability about Calvary; but it is not isolated or solitary. It is a decisive enactment of the world's continuing rejection of its own good and at the same time a decisive enactment of God's unfailing and never-ceasing participation in the affairs of the creation. There was enormous insight in a remark of Charles A. Dinsmore, an American theologian of an earlier generation, who said that from all eternity "there has been a Cross at the heart of God." Likewise, there is enormous insight in the saying of Thomas Chalmers, the Scots theologian, that what is required to meet men and women in their human wrongness and deliver them from that condition is "the expulsive power of a new affection."

But there is also something else to be said. If God is indeed affected by what happens in the creation, then the obedient self-giving of Jesus to the point of death has made a difference *in God himself*. By this I do not mean that God has become loving after having been only just; I do not mean that there is any change in the continuing nature and loving activity of God as sheer Love-in-act. What I am trying to get at is that once this focal event has taken place in the creation, God has possibilities of relationship with us human children which previously and otherwise God could not have possessed without denying to them their freedom, dignity and responsibility. Once this event happened, God's ability to relate to and act in the human realm acquired a genuinely new outlet.

And what is that outlet? Simply that what we who are of the Christian fellowship describe as "life in Christ," in a community whose animating principle is the "love of God in Christ Jesus our Lord," is now available in such a fashion that it makes a real difference. Not that God does not always do "the best God can" for any and every creature; to talk in that fashion would be to deny that God is sheer Love. Rather, there is now an intensification (so to say) of that ceaseless concern and care. On the *divine* side this is made possible precisely because what takes place in the world both matters to God and has its consequence in God and for God. On the *human* side, as men and women are caught up in the love which, in the event of Christ, has been "let loose" into their situation, there is now available an intensification of the possibility of profound response in faith, obedience and a returning love towards God—and also, as a consequence, in "love for the brethren."

What has been said previously about human lovelessness and human inability to love and return love is equally true when we consider our human alienation and estrangement, along with our incapacity to accept ourselves. We are concerned here, of course, with what in a preceding chapter we saw to be Paul Tillich's way of interpreting God's deliverance of us human children. It is impossible for us, of and by ourselves, to overcome this alienation from our true possibility in relationship with God; it is impossible for us, of and by ourselves, to alter our state of estrangement from that human possibility and from God who purposes it for us. It is impossible for us to accept ourselves, "just as we are," for it is precisely our condition of felt unacceptability which creates the great obstacle. To use a familiar idiom, there are "barriers" between God and us, as also between brother and brother and sister and sister in human community, which nothing on our part alone can break down or destroy. The more we try the more we fail. An attempt to lift ourselves by our own bootstraps is bound to fail. Whatever theories we may have about this, the fact of it is plain enough to anyone of us.

But in the Cross of Christ, where divine Love was both disclosed and released, something happened which changed this situation. The well-known gospel hymn puts it admirably: "Just as I am, thy Love unknown/hath broken every barrier down. . . ." *God* has done this: it is for us *humans* to respond. The now-open channel for response is made available for us through Christ, "through the veil of his flesh" given to the point of death. The barriers were set up by us humans and not by God. They are nothing other than our self-centering and our unwillingness to act in a fashion which says "Amen" or "So be it" to the divine loving initiative. *God* has destroyed the barriers which we have set up by his self-identification with us in Christ, vividly "placarded" (as St. Paul puts it) on Calvary. The estrangement is overcome and the alienation taken away. Humans can now accept themselves and can accept others because God accepts them and welcomes them into a free fellowship.

A final point should be made here. The Christian can never see Calvary without its tranfiguration by Easter Day. In Christian faith, Good Friday and Easter morning go together. The God who was active in the event of Christ is the God who in that event demonstrated the reality of the divine nature as love. This is also the God who made plain to us the enormity of our human sinning. But at the same time God overcame that sinning by victory over it. What is more, this is the God who in the crucifixion of Jesus Christ showed the true nature of that divine victory over wrong. We might even say that Good Friday and Easter (taken together) are two sides of the same reality.

The love which was demonstrated on Calvary is the love that nothing can destroy: it "cannot be holden of death" nor of anything else which seeks to deny it. The Easter victory is the assurance that this human loving, which was Jesus, is now part of the reality of God. It has been accepted and received into the divine life and hence "raised from the dead." But it has also been released or (as I have frequently phrased it in this book) "let loose" into the world of men and women, so that it may grasp them and use them for its own ends—and these ends are the ever wider sharing of love and loving by more people in more places in more ways at more times. And as I have argued, the Process conceptuality assists us here by providing a context in which this Christian experience, with its biblical grounding, may be given a proper setting appropriate to the apostolic witness and to succeeding Christian sensibility and also credible and intelligible in our own time.

We now turn to look at traditional talk about justification and sanctification. Unhappily, many theologians have made these two into entirely distinct and sometimes even separate workings of God. Of course, as we shall see, there is a sense in which a distinction may be made;

but any talk of *absolute* distinction or complete separation is essentially a denial of the processive quality of our human existence. John Wesley, it appears, was practically ready to assimilate justification to sanctification. If he did do this, he was surely thinking along the right lines. For since sanctification means the conforming of human existence to the divine purpose or intention, towards the image of God, then justification is appropriately understood as the first step along that path, a path which was styled "the process of Christ" by William Law (a writer much admired by John Wesley) in one of his essays in *The Christian Life*. We have to do with a movement on the human side which responds to the prior movement towards us on God's part. And it is all of a piece.

In theological circles there has been considerable disagreement about how we can best interpret the notion of justification. On the one hand most of those who are followers of the Reformation, with its appeal to the *ipsissima verba* of Scripture, have insisted that the only proper meaning of justification is to be found in an almost literal acceptance of some of St. Paul's remarks in his epistles, where he often seems to be thinking about our "being declared" righteous or "accounted as" righteous by God because of what was accomplished in Jesus Christ. It is something that is done *to* us and *for* us by God's fiat. On the other hand, most Catholic theologians have not been prepared to make such an exclusive appeal to the supposedly Pauline view, but have interpreted justification in the light of the general tenor of biblical teaching; often here with particular attention, perhaps, to the way in which in Johannine writing the point seems to be made. Thus for them we are not only declared to be righteous; we are *made righteous* through God's act in Christ: "made" righteous, that is, in the sense that we are enabled through this act to begin a process of responding to God who accepts us as already being what we hope to become. And this acceptance takes place despite our falling far short of our intended destiny. With this Catholic position it is natural that there has also been a greater emphasis on sanctification as necessarily the significant part of the total movement.

As the word indicates, sanctification means "being made holy"—becoming like Christ, thanks to the action of the divine Spirit released in Christ, as the Spirit works in the believer. Those who make a sharp separation between justification and sanctification usually say that the former is the first and essential step. By virtue of their justification sinful human beings are thought to have been turned to God from their wrongness; and by their committing themselves in faith to Christ are now accounted to be in the right, although this does not necessarily imply that they *feel* this justification. Once they have been declared by God to be "righteous before him" through Christ's act, they may then experience sanctification as they grow in grace and are able "to follow the blessed steps of [Christ's] most holy life." This is a slow and painful experience. The "old Adam" has to die, so that the "new Adam," or the Christ-nature, may develop and grow in the believer. But need we make such a separation between justification and sanctification?

My contention is that we shall not get any proper notion of what this is all about if we seek simply to follow some supposedly plain bit of New Testament teaching such as that found chiefly in the Pauline epistles. I believe the better course is to grasp first what in a large and comprehensive way the New Testament witness is getting at; and second, to attempt to see how in actual Christian living the process of deliverance works itself out in the faithful believer.

As to the first, it is sufficient to say that with a great variety of emphasis and expression, the witness found in the New Testament tells us that the event of Jesus Christ, climaxed in his death and resurrection, makes what I have earlier styled *a difference*. The difference is not only in respect to human possibility, but also in the making available to God of what was accomplished in Christ's death and rising again. Here is new material which God may now employ in his dealings with his children. The divine attitude and concern, of course, remain constant; but the adaptation of these to the concrete situations in which men and women find themselves will differ both because of those actual situations and also because of what has been "determined, dared and done" in Christ. But the continuing mutual relationship between God and humans is integral to this picture; and its importance ought not to be forgotten when we speak of the "difference" which has been made by the specific historical occurrence which we call Christ.

Thus whose who respond to the "placarding" of God's love, along with the release of that love for human existence—both of which are given in Jesus Christ—are not only put on the right path towards full and proper human actuality. They are also "treated" by God as having already become what, in the divine intention, they are always meant to become: men and women "in Christ"; men and women whose existence is grounded in the divine Love made humanly visible and available. To greater or lesser degree they become conscious of what is made possible for them. Thus justification and sanctification belong together.

The teaching of John Wesley resembled the Catholic view that the more inclusive aspect of the process is sanctification: the making of men and women into Christ's likeness by their responsive action as God provides more and more opportunities for human existence to become, in some genuine sense, "partaker of the divine nature." The Fathers of the Church used to speak of God's "becoming human" so that humans might "become divine." By this they did not intend for a moment to suggest that a human being could literally "become divine"; their purpose was to point to a genuine sharing in God's life, given for men to know and love, to receive and express, so that in the end what William Law called "the process of Christ" might be brought to completion in them.

We can now see the significance of still another insight of John Wesley, for which he has been often either condemned or severely criticized. This has to do with "perfection" as a possibility for a devout believer. If we take into account the processive aspect of human existence, we can readily discern what Wesley was getting at. To be "living in love," which means living in God who is Love, is already, in however limited a way, to be "perfected." Let us remember here that "perfection," as found in the words attributed to Jesus in the Sermon on the Mount—"Be ye perfect *(teleioi)* as your heavenly Father is perfect *(teleios)*"—means to become what we are intended to be, to the limit of our human capacity. This has nothing to do with some "ideal" notion of perfection, untouched by the "changes and chances" of mortal life. Rather it is growth in love and in loving, which can only come when human life is on the right path, turned from wrong and turned towards good, and zealously responding to the divine call so far as this can be done under given finite circumstances.

Our discussion up to this point has prepared us for attention to the significance of human sinning in the concrete and particular ways in which, as a matter of fact, men and women obviously fail to be their true divinely purposed selves in community with their fellows. Something must be said about those "sins" (in the plural) which are expressions or manifestations of the wrongness or "sin" (in the singular) from which (in response to the event of Christ) humans are said by Christian faith to be delivered, and also about that basic wrongness we discussed in a preceding chapter.

Our concern here is not with a listing of specific sins, such as is often found in popular books of devotion written to assist believers in preparing themselves for confession to an ordained priest. Neither is it with such questions as the distinction between so-called "mortal sins," or those of a specially grievous nature, and so-called "venial sins," which are less grievous in nature (which is traditional in moral theology). Rather, I wish to make the point that particular instances of sin—this or that particular thought or word or deed which we designate by speaking of "sins"—have their primary importance in that they indicate, positively or negatively, whether a man or woman is in fact responding so far as possible to the lure towards fulfillment which God provides in all the varying occasions of human life. We can become so interested in the details of sins in and of themselves that this more significant aspect is forgotten. It is possible to spend our time weighing the "gravity" of sins, and thus devote our attention to the enterprise of avoiding them, so that the question of the routing or direction of life is neglected. Whatever else may be said about the sins of which people are guilty, either by omission or commission, their theological significance is surely in their indication of the direction or routing of life which is expressed in these specific ways.

Hence we should ask what such particular sins in fact show about the man or woman who is in question. In what way and to what degree, we should inquire, is this or that person so much in a condition of lovelessness, in alienation from the truest self, in estrangement from the God who invites response, and in awareness of unacceptability, that he or she simply cannot find a way to move forward towards the "mark of his [her] high calling"; that is, to repent and move once again towards the realization or actualization of the movement towards reflecting and serving as a personalized instrument for divine Love-in-act. If the destiny towards which each of us should be moving is indeed to reflect that image and to become instrumental in the service of the God whose image it is, we need always to be brought to a real awareness of our concrete human situation. Only then will it be possible for us, on our part, to accept the forgiveness of God. And that forgiveness is not so much a matter of obliterating past actions, words or thoughts, as it is a matter of the divine acceptance of us "just as we are," with the readiness on God's part to surround us with help. In more conventional language, God constantly makes available for us the grace (or divine favor and assistance) which alone can enable us to move forward towards and in the human perfection which God intends for us.

It is here, of course, that the fact of the Cross has its particularly vivid place in our consciousness. To look at the Cross and then to look at ourselves is to be shamed by what we see our condition to be. "If God so loved us," we must ask, "how do we so terribly fail to be the sort of persons whom God *can* love?" To be sure, we know that God loves us despite our failures. The point is that we do not always realize how badly we have failed and how much we are in need of making our response to that love if our lives are to be set on the right path. This is the subjective side, which Abelard stressed but without losing sight fo the divine and objective side. It is also the emphasis which is found in what is sometimes called the "moral theory of atonement." Often enough, in our perfectly correct wish to stress objectivity here, we forget that in a two-movement like that between God and his world the subjective side is of equal significance with the objective. Hence I urge that an awareness of our particular occasions of sin, of this and that wrong because of an unloving word or thought or deed, will have its vital part in making the Cross of Christ a telling reality in our lives.

Years ago my old teacher William Adams Brown made an interesting comment in one of his lectures, using familiar hymns to illustrate it. He said that in Christian faith there is always a stress on what one hymn calls the "green hill" where Jesus died on the Cross. So in another hymn we sing, "In the cross of Christ I glory." And rightly so. We also sing that "when we survey the wondrous Cross" we are moved to count our human gains as only "loss." But we should always remember, he said, the old gospel hymn which says that "There's a cross for everyone/And there's a cross for me." In other words, one of the experiences that brings Calvary home to each of us is the realization that we need "to be crucified" to the things which have built and still build barriers between God and us. Consciousness of sin as a condition, but above all consciousness of the particular sins which we have committed and do commit, will make us more profoundly aware of the "awful sinfulness of sin." Hence we shall be moved again and again to the repentance which alone can give God an entrance into our lives. Yet that is not the right way to phrase it, since our real repentance can take place only *after* we have known that God is sheer Love-in-act who moves ceaselessly and unfailingly out towards us. Because God is like the father to the prodigal son in Jesus' parable, we see ourselves as we are. Our repentance is awakened and gradually becomes more real and more complete.

In this chapter I have sought to make plain that Christian life, freed to love by the deliverance made available in the event of Jesus Christ, has many facets. Above all, it is not a matter of something over and done with. It is an ongoing movement in which the initiative is always with God. Yet that initiative cannot accomplish its aim until and unless there is a genuine response on the part of the person. The movement is from God to us who are God's human children and from us human children back to God. Once more the Process conceptuality is of value in providing the sort of broad context in which the biblical witness and the testimony of human experience can find their proper place.

I must repeat here—to avoid any misunderstanding—what I said in the first chapters. I do not for a moment think that the Process conceptuality (or any other conceptuality) is identical with or can be made into a substitute for the affirmations of Christian faith. That faith has its own integrity; it has what might even be called a certain independence from any and every philosophical position. At the same time, however, whenever the faith is stated theologically, some conceptuality will inevitably be present. The reason for this is simply that when men and women make any statement (save perhaps about the most trivial and insignificant matters) they presuppose a view of the world, of how things go in the world, and of their own human existence. They may not be vividly conscious of their presuppositions; indeed, often they may not be conscious of them at all. Nonetheless, they do necessarily entertain some set of ideas, some view of the world and of themselves. If they did not do this, they would not be in the situation in which they find themselves with a capacity for human awareness and thought. That situation makes both possible and necessary a context for any statement; and it is also implicit in the way in which the statement is made.

In the context of the Christian awareness of redemption or deliverance, therefore, my point in arguing for the use of the Process conceptuality is not its indispensability nor its identification with Christian affirmations of faith. To talk that way would be absurd. Rather, my point is that among the available ways of interpreting our human experience in a world such as we now know ours to be, this seems to me the most suitable and adequate. It has no absolute quality. It is clearly corrigible and it may very well be superseded in some later period. After all, finite human beings can hardly be said to have access to the complete "truth" about things as that truth in fact exists. The best that they can hope for is a sufficient adequacy to what they know and experience. I believe that the Process conceptuality which I use is, to that extent, adequate.

Furthermore, this conceptuality is also sufficiently in tune with the general understanding which finds expression in the Scriptures to make it especially appealing to a theologian. To be sure, the biblical way of talking about the world and about God and God's human children is not philosophical in nature. The Bible does not make metaphysical assertions; evidently the Hebrew mind did not function in that fashion. *We* might speak of the divine transcendence; *the Bible* will say that "God sitteth above the waterfloods; he remaineth a king for ever." *We* might say that this transcendent reality is participant in human affairs through immanence and inspiration; *the Bible* will talk about "the high and holy one who inhabiteth eternity" but yet "is with those who are of a humble and contrite heart." So we could go on, with thousands of possible examples readily at hand to make the point. But granted this difference in language, it remains true that the general biblical outlook—with its stress on divine activity, on the created order as open to God's working, on the divine nature discerned through a long historical development as holy love, on human existence as finite and defective yet meant to be "in God's image," on human freedom and responsibility—is *more like* the kind of world view which is proposed in Process Thought than like a portrayal of God as immutable substance, impassible, self-contained and self-sufficient, without necessary relationship to the creation, and with no possibility of being affected or influenced by what goes on in that creation.

There is a final point. If the Cross is indeed "crucial" in the picture, if human existence receives deliverance from God through the event of Christ and above all through what was "done" on Calvary, what about the millions of humans who have no knowledge of, or who find themselves unable to respond to, that event? The decisive nature of the event of Christ and the crucial significance of Calvary must not be taken as setting up an exclusivist theology in which *only* by a conscious response to them is deliverance possible. There have been some who have talked in that fashion. Many of today's conservative evangelicals still do so. In the very week that I am writing this chapter I have been sent a review of an earlier book of mine in which the reviewer, who is a conservatively minded evangelical American, said that the grave defect of my book was that I failed to stress the absolute necessity of response, consciously made in self-surrender and commitment, to the historical figure of Jesus of Nazareth accepted as divine Savior. For him, those who do not make that kind of response cannot be regarded as "saved." But to me such a view makes nonsense of Christian faith in God as Love. The deity who is portrayed in that view to my mind bears little resemblance to "the God and Father of our Lord Jesus Christ." I think the view is both unChristian and incredible.

I realize that to put it so bluntly as that may seem to be arrogant and presumptuous. But I do not apologize for saying this, since I have increasingly become convinced that one of the barriers for a great many people in their attitude to Christian faith is precisely to be found in that narrowly christocentric attitude which appears to *them* to be even more presumptuous and indeed absurd than it does to me. Furthermore, they are in the position which many years ago Whitehead stated so succinctly when he said that *if* men and women today are to make any sense of belief in God it must be through the insistence that God is *not* so exclusive in attitude as some of those who say they believe in him, but rather through a presentation of deity in terms of unfailing love. The gospel is an "offense," to use St. Paul's word, to those who are centered upon themselves and who are victims of all-too-human pride and the desire to have the world revolve around their own interests. It is *not* "offensive" in the sense that it outrages moral sensibility and seems to be all-too-ready to condemn and reject persons who cannot accept pretentious claims to the exclusive possession of divine favor.

It is too bad that there are still far too many people who profess and call themselves by the Christian name but are unwilling to show the generosity of spirit and the delight in good wherever found, which one would have taken to be the mark of genuine Christian faith in a divine reality whose love is universal in its scope even as it is particular in its application. The "liberty of the children of God," of which St. Paul writes, ought to be such that it can recognize and accept gladly those whose way of response to divine initiative is not their own. Hence I claim, with boldness but with confidence, that God works in many ways, both within and apart from the specifically Christian commitment, to bring sons and daughters of humankind to freedom. God's great purpose is to make it possible for *all* of us to be enabled to live in love, with the concern for human justice and the urgent striving for release from all manner of oppression which are the inevitable corollaries of that love.

This brings us to the question of liberation theology and its relationship to what has so far been urged in this book.

6

Redemption and Liberation

Anyone who follows news from the Third World is aware of the extraordinary impact which is now being made, at first in African countries but now particularly in Latin America, by the movement which is called Liberation Theology. But the movement is found elsewhere as well, notably in the United States where it has received the support of many in the black community as well as in numerous feminist groups and in the increasingly large homosexual associations, which include the Metropolitan Community Church. The last of these was founded about twenty years ago by a young American clergyman of evangelical antecedents, Troy Perry, and now numbers perhaps a hundred thousand men and women in local churches all over the United States. (Some are even in England and on the continents of Europe and Australasia.) All these people, responding to some remarkably able theologians in Latin America, Europe and the United States, insist that the Christian gospel has a direct relevance to those who are underprivileged by reason of their background in poverty, because of their race or color, because they belong to the female sex, or because as homosexuals they have felt ostracized and even rejected by traditional Christian bodies.

It goes without saying that anybody who is concerned for the gospel's proclamation that through the event of Jesus Christ men and women have been "freed to love," as I have put it in this book, must be in profound sympathy with these liberation movements. As I have said again and again, genuine human loving entails a readiness to work for justice in every aspect of human existence, to seek to overcome oppression of whatever sort, and to support those who are struggling to secure for themselves and for others the right to the fullest possible expression of their humanness as persons made "towards God's image" and meant by God to grow to the "measure of the stature of the fullness of Christ." At the same time, it is necessary to look carefully at Liberation Theology, and its associated practical action, in order to see how it supplements and completes, but does not replace, the age-old Christian concern for the redemption of humankind in the ways we have been discussing.

To some readers it may seem that much which has been said in earlier pages was concerned with *persons*—and that is indeed the case. But in the Process conceptuality there is no such thing as a "person" without social relationships or "belonging." This conceptuality makes it inevitable that whatever is said about any one of us is bound to be said of us in our concrete existence as participants in the human race, not to mention the equally significant fact that we are also, by necessity, participants in the entire created order as it makes its "advance" in a mutual relationship with God. And it is also true that the biblical presentation of human existence demands the same sort of social belonging as integral to humankind. Unhappily there is no such guarantee in much of the philosophical-theological outlook that has been dominant for many centuries in western Christianity, although, of course, the Christian tradition has always stressed precisely such participation of each of us in the total human situation and hence with our sisters and brothers in the human enterprise.

Thus it should have been clear that whatever idiom I have been using in the discussion of redemption, I am very far from supporting the notion of "individual salvation" as this has commonly been preached and taught in certain Christian groups. It is tragic that much post-Reformation discussion has seemed to speak in that fashion; and above all, it is sad that a good deal of evangelism, not least in recent years, has been undertaken in that vein. When I hear a street-corner preacher—as I did recently in Cambridge—exhorting those who stop to listen to him, I am appalled by the way in which so frequently an appeal is being made to what at best can be styled as "enlightened self-interest" and at worst as a *sauve qui peut* concern for individualistically conceived salvation. This is a parody of genuine Christian faith and practice. And while it may be understandable, in the sense that there *are* men and women who more readily respond to such an extrication-theology, that does not make such preaching other than a frightful distortion of the wholeness of the authentic Christian vision of God's purpose and way with human life.

At the same time, however, it must be admitted that the broader Christian affirmation has often been forgotten; and it must also be granted that the implications of that affirmation, in political, economic and other areas of human existence, have not always—perhaps have not often—been recognized and stressed. In the days when the so-called social gospel was being taught, this was not the case. But in that period, there was often an almost exact identification of Christianity as a whole with these implications, so that it might have seemed that to be a Christian meant primarily to work for social justice in its various aspects. What is more, there was also a tendency to accept a highly optimistic view of human affairs, such that it was assumed by many of the "social gospelers" that it would be possible, through devoted human effort, to "build the kingdom of God in this world." Thus there was a secularization, in the pejorative sense, of the gospel message and a confusion of God's kingdom with an earthly utopia, taken to be the "divine event to which the whole creation moved"— and moved in what appeared to be an almost automatic fashion.

In reaction to this perversion of Christian understanding, there has often been a revulsion on the part of Christian theologians from the notion of social action and an emphasis upon what I have just styled "individualistic salvation." From that overreaction present-day liberation thinking is delivering us. No longer is it possible for thoughtful Christian men and women to be blind to the patent truth that precisely because all of us are by the very nature of our human existence participants in a social cosmos, there is an obligation to work towards the changing of the world in every area. To be "saved," to be "freed to love," requires of us a devotion to the welfare of others and a liberation for them from whatever it is that oppresses them or denies them their human rights; and with this devotion there must be a concern to establish in this world not the kingdom of God (which is not to be achieved by human effort and is always a gift of God and hence has an "eschatological" quality) but such a state of affairs as shall promote, as adequately and fully as is possible under finite (because human) conditions, genuine freedom for everyone—and for everyone in the most complete human sense.

This is not the place, nor have I the knowledge, for a full statement of all that is involved in this enterprise as part of Christian discipleship in response to the prevenient love of God with its corollary in the divine justice. There are many different aspects of the enterprise, and we should be grateful that in our own day these are increasingly recognized and discussed. Yet, as I said at the beginning of this chapter, it is not that the wider social implications of human redemption replace, or take over from, whatever must be said about redemption as deliverance from human sin and about obedience to the divine will by each of us. My worry is that sometimes the advocates of Liberation Theology appear to think that this perennial affirmation, with the experience which follows upon it, may be shoved to one side, with all Christian effort being directed to the political, economic and other kinds of human freedom which in some sense may be considered as "social."

In other words, I agree with Schubert Ogden and others who have insisted that there are two aspects of the redemptive movement. One of them is indeed the wider social concern, while the other is the recognition that in our being social we are also necessarily "personal." This demands that each one of us shall be "redeemed" from all that would prevent the fullest realization of his or her personal selfhood as a child of God. For it remains true, and will always be true, that every man and woman is loved by God for himself or herself—not only as one given instance of the common sociality which is ours by nature, but also in his or her concrete "personal" existence.

"We die alone," said Martin Luther, and perhaps that may stand as an indication of the plain fact that each one of us *counts* as a person and must be seen to be such; each counts for God quite as much as for fellow humans. The most perfect human society, where all impediments to freedom seem to have been removed, cannot provide the answer to the highly "personal" question: "What do I mean and what value do I have, as this distinctive and particular human person, in the total scheme of things?" And with this there is the related

question, "Is there a way in which this personal worth may be
guaranteed, so that I can come to see and know that I am indeed
delivered from a condition of lovelessness, loneliness and alienation,
into the liberty of God's sons and daughters?"

We have here another occasion when we dare not talk in "either-
or" terms but must always speak and think *and act* in "both-and" ways.
Both a concern for human sociality and a concern for human personality are required. Either one without the other is to my mind a
frightening denial of the integral Christian vision of human redemption.

First of all, then, we need to see that love and justice are not
in conflict in any soundly based interpretation of how things go in
the world. There have been some Christian thinkers—for example
Emil Brunner in one or two of his books—who appear to believe that
love is a matter of personal relationships in a somewhat narrow "I-
thou" sense, while justice is another business, however important it
may be. There have also been others, usually not Christians to be
sure, but who are nonetheless representative of a profound social
awareness, who have talked as if justice could be regarded as careless
of the given person and that it has reference only to states of affairs
in a highly abstract way. Both of these views seem to me to be
dangerously erroneous. If I truly love others, even if I truly love *one*
other, I am by necessity put in the position where I must strive for
that other's best good, which will inevitably include deliverance from
all that stands in the way of his or her achievement of fullness of
life. On the other hand, if I am heartily dedicated to the accomplishment of a society which is genuinely just, I need to see that such
a society is made up of persons, each of them in his or her integrity,
each of them a loved child of God, so that there is always a movement
towards and a "personalized" concern for them; not "in the mass" but
as truly this or that or the other *one*, whose welfare is to be sought
and for whom, both as persons and as persons-in-relationship, I am
to give myself wholeheartedly and for whose fulfillment I am to do
all in my power. My aim, then, is neither "rugged individualism"
nor "ant-hill community," but a genuine common life in which (as
an old prayer puts it) "each cares for all and all care for each." That
is to say, the way in which *love* works is with and for persons-in-
the-making; and the way in which *justice* works is to bring to such

persons-in-the-making the opportunities which are necessary if human life, here and now, is to be lived in love, by love and with love.

People may often labor for justice in a highly impersonal fashion, interested only in making such adjustments or promoting such revolutionary change as may seem right to them, but without any serious personal involvement. But it is more likely that what they decide to do rests back upon some kind of genuine concern. This need not be emotional, to be sure; it may often seem to be somewhat chilly in its expression. Yet it is highly likely that the majority of men and women respond to something not unlike John Woolman's "concern laid upon his heart" (as that remarkable early American campaigner for the abolition of slavery put it). That is to say, they are distressed at what seems to be nothing other than wicked oppression of those who for one reason or another are not able to stand up for themselves and hence are victimized by others, not least by people who are in the position to dominate society at any given time or place. Thus justice is not only closely associated with love in the more obvious sense; love is also frequently, if not always, the motivating power which brings them to seek for and work towards a just state of affairs. What is more, at times when "the going is hard," it is the persistence of such concern, which is a manifestation of love in some degree high or low, that persuades them to carry on when opposition arises or when they are subject to misunderstanding or misrepresentation.

In the second place, as far as I can see, there are no specific Christian details about how such justice is to be achieved. In a broad sense, certainly, there is a Christian view which teaches that each and every human life should be helped to mature, with suitable opportunities provided for this maturing, with no obstacles created beyond those inevitably attaching to human finitude and to the limitations of human knowledge, and with no special privileges given to any class or group or even to any person. The aim is to secure such an ordering of social existence, in its every aspect, as shall make this maturing possible. This is why slavery, deprivation, rejection because of race or color or sexual orientation or family background or situation, as well as anything else which interferes with healthy and sound human growth, is to be condemned. It is also why political life must be related to the welfare of the whole people and why conflicts, within a given society or among nations, are to be resolved without unnecessary violence, warfare or domination of one group or class or nation over others. And differing circumstances alter things, so that (for example) the concept of a "just war" is no longer a meaningful idea, whatever may have been the case at earlier times. When Pope John Paul II speaks boldly against all these forms of political, social, economic and other modes of oppression of the poor, needy, rejected, neglected and outcast men and women of any nation, he is saying exactly what the Christian conscience must necessarily require him to say.

Yet when this is granted, we need also to see that particular platforms or projects, programs or movements, are not in themselves the point. Such are essential if anything is to be accomplished; but it is absurd to assume that there is a specifically Christian political party, or Christian program for social action, or Christian fashion in which the ends in view must necessarily be achieved. Here there is room for plenty of difference of opinion. What is important is that those who are expert in the study of economics, for example, shall be called in to advise and help. Likewise persons who are competent in political affairs are needed to suggest how best the goal of a truly egalitarian political structure may be reached. Hence devoted Christian people, who know that freedom to love demands also freedom to live, need not always be supporters of (say, in the British scene) Labor Party policies. They may perfectly well be "conservatives with a conscience," as it has been phrased; or they may belong to no particular party or pressure group, but be ready to support whatever proposals or actions seem to them at the time to promise most for the achievement of the free society which a Christian must seek.

This means that any Christian ought to have what Bishop Charles Gore urged, "a permanently troubled conscience," whenever or wherever he or she sees stark injustice. That carries with it the requirement that such a Christian should also have an *informed* conscience, which is to say that he or she should not be ready to accept whatever may happen to be the present state of affairs when that state of affairs plainly entails oppression. No Christian can contemplate with equanimity the way in which black people in many countries (not only in South Africa, although there the situation is appallingly obvious) are denied elemental human rights. Or, to take a more touchy matter, a Christian ought not to acquiesce in the refusal of civil justice—in terms of right to employment, opportunity for housing, chance of getting a job, etc.—to men and women who, because of their homosexual orientation, are unlike the great majority of their fellow citizens in any country or city or organization. Again, no Christian can be content to see the expenditure of vast sums of money, by any government or group, for the support of oppressive regimes. But just how remedies are to be found for all these forms of injustice is a matter to be worked out; it is not divinely revealed to anybody, not even to the leaders of the great institutional churches, who sometimes are expected to dictate precisely how and when, and with what specific measures, legal or otherwise, the rights of men and women are to be guaranteed (or, when they have been denied, to be reasserted).

When Whitehead wrote that the aim or intention basic to the world is making possible for men and women "to live, to live well, and to live better," he was voicing a secularized version of this basic Christian insight. Human effort, he said, is to be directed towards that end and he was prepared to affirm that so to act is to behave in accordance with what he styled "the grain of the universe." A Christian will assent to this; but a Christian will also say that this is but a rephrasing of the fact that God's will or purpose or intent is precisely to bring about just this situation. He will add that men and women are called to cooperate with the divine reality, as its reflection and its instruments, towards that end. To fail here is to succumb to the temptation to sin, since sin (as I have urged throughout this book) is nothing other than a violation or breaking of those relationships (between God and humankind and among men and women) that in fact promote the possibility of living, living well, and the desire to live better, which is the reflection of the divine purpose for the human creation.

Again, it must be recognized that the results of an acceptance of injustice are felt not only by the oppressed but by the oppressors. In a serious way, although not always an obvious one, those who behave unjustly towards others suffer the consequences. Their own existence is narrowed, cheapened and in the long run endangered by their blindness and obstinacy, quite as much as by their overt actions in behaving oppressively to others, above all to those who so readily become their unwilling or willing subjects because of their powerlessness in to fight back.

This leads to the issue of violence. A few of those who are advocates of Liberation Theology seem to be unable to recognize that the use of violent means to secure good ends is likely to be self-defeating in the long run. Most, however, do insist that it is only in the last resort, when all more peaceful methods are of no avail, that a measure of violent action may be indicated. But just as wars never really settle problems, but only succeed in creating new (and perhaps more serious) ones, so in other ways, too, the ready use of violence is likely to breed hatred, contempt and anger which often enough redound on those who use such violence. In the Middle Ages, regicide was considered to be the very last resort of those who sought to overthrow tyrannical rulers. It was never to be recommended as a consistent policy to be adopted whenever such a tyrant came to power, but only after every other available means had been sought to remove such a person from high position. This principle is applicable today, quite as much as in earlier times. Revolutions may be necessary, if tyranny is to be overcome; but that does not mean that revolution must be achieved by bloodshed and its accompaniments. In a world like ours, nobody's hands are entirely clean. That is a part of our common involvement in a state of affairs in which through millennia of wrong choices (and their consequences), as well as through wrong decisions made today by each one for himself or herself, things are not as they ought to be—as they ought to be if and as human interest is dedicated to the securing of fullness of life for everybody. To recognize that this is tragically true, however, is not at the same time to approve the dirtying of human hands beyond necessity. William Occam's "razor" applies here as elsewhere.

Sometimes the most effective way to work for such necessary changes as will provide better living is through passive resistance, like that of Gandhi and his followers in India in the days before independence was granted the people of that subcontinent. So also Martin Luther King in the United States contended that the most satisfactory and successful achievement of rights for the black population of that country would be by continued, persistent and devoted witness and action, but without the shedding of blood. In many ways such a policy is more difficult to advocate and more difficult to carry out than violent action that might seem to grant almost instant results. Yet for a Christian such as King, and for a profoundly religious man of another faith like Gandhi, this was the only way. Any other way was for them untrue to the deepest insight of those who, because of their deep faith, are sure that the divine reality is essentially Love-in-act, not sheer power at work in the world.

For such leaders the call was to be loyal to that insight and, if necessary, to suffer for it; but then it was also their conviction—and for a Christian who has been made free to live in love this above all must be the case—that this same divine reality is itself (himself or herself, if we wish to use personalizing terms) prepared to suffer and indeed does suffer along with the sons and daughters of the human race. Often the most effectual action is that sort of passion: a fellow-suffering which shames the oppressors, provides comfort and solace for the oppressed, and in the long run (which may indeed be a very long run) can bring to both a genuine participation in a society where love and justice go hand and hand.

I realize that the discussion in this chapter is brief and to some may seem incredibly "optimistic." I am sure, however, that the optimism is realistic, provided we are ready to see that God is truly Love-in-act and that we humans have been given deliverance from our lovelessness, loneliness, alienation, and non-acceptability by the gracious action of God "for us humans and for our salvation." We must see "salvation" as both personal and social—and social precisely because it is personal.

7

The Loving Community

In a remarkably interesting essay published in the book *Christ For Us Today* (SCM Press, 1968), a volume containing the addresses given at the Modern Churchmen's Conference in Oxford in 1967, Dr. Dennis Nineham wrote as follows: "God was seeking to do through Jesus what he has in fact done, bring into existence a community under the lordship of the Risen One, in which reconciliation with God himself and the power of a holy life should become, at least potentially, a reality" (pp. 64-5). In these words Dr. Nineham put succinctly what I have been urging in the present book. The event of Jesus Christ, in disclosing and releasing the divine Love into the affairs of humankind, had as its consequence the emergence in the realm of human history of a social process, whose existence is the effectual working-out—within the limits imposed by human finitude—of God's purpose to establish a relationship with men and women in which a responding love is made to the prevenient divine loving, and a "holy life" (one that is moving in the right direction "towards the image of God" and hence marked by the power of love) is made possible for those same human children. In other words, the Christian community, the Church, is essentially "the loving community," in which there is deliverance from lovelessness, loneliness, the feeling of unacceptability and the sense of alienation and estrangement. In sharing in that communal existence, which is the Church, men and women are "freed to love."

Now it is obviously true that in a great many ways the Christian

Church as we see it and know it bears little resemblance to what I have just been urging. Simple honesty compels us to say that much of the time the Church appears a narrow, introverted, self-serving institution, whose major concern seems to be its own preservation and aggrandizement. What has been called "the empirical Church" can often seem to be only a caricature of the blessed community about which Dr. Nineham wrote and about which I have been writing in this book.

Yet that is not all there is to say about the Christian Church. Often, in hidden ways, it has conveyed to succeeding generations the proclamation of the originative event of Jesus Christ and has managed to communicate to millions of men and women the reality of divine Love and the energizing power of that same Love for human living. Furthermore, it is the Church which has conveyed the given data to which the apostolic witness was borne and which has made the figure of Jesus Christ a fact to be recognized and acknowledged even by those who disclaim any specific Christian allegiance. To put it bluntly, the Church seems to have two aspects. One is the plainly visible and not always very inspiring aspect which we indicate when we speak of the institutional or hierarchical society; the other is the "stream of influence" (to use once again Whitehead's telling language) in which the consequences of the event of Jesus Christ are effectual in the realm of human history from the earliest days up to the present moment.

In this chapter I shall endeavor to portray the Church in its God-intended reality—not an "invisible Church," which somehow subsists in and behind the visible society which we encounter every day where we live, but rather one that exists precisely in and under the conditions of human, mortal and finite existence. There are defects that mark that existence, which men and women in our own time, as in every earlier time, have encountered. Sometimes, indeed, it seems necessary to "hate" the institution in order to come to this churchly reality in its divine meaning. Any "triumphalism" about the institution and its ways is a scandalous thing. As Vatican II made clear, the Church is always being reformed so that it can more adequately represent, stand for and impart the love of God in Christ Jesus and can more suitably and properly serve as the agency for the divine Love directed towards the creation. Thus, as in an earlier piece of writing I once ventured to remark, one must learn "to put up with the Church [as an institution] in order to love the Church [as the pilgrim community] in its 'mystery' as 'the Body of Christ.' "

Our major interest in the discussion which follows is not with the failure of the organized Christian community to live up to its basic mission. Rather it is with the ways in which freedom from the condition of loveless existence, the state of loneliness, alienation from fulfillment, estrangement from God and other humans, and the tragic feeling of human unacceptability has been made available through the Christian fellowship. This will require us to consider what is usually styled "the nature of the Church," with its several "notes" of unity, holiness, catholicity and apostolicity; with attention to related matters such as the general ministry belonging to all members of the Church; and with the place of *ordained* ministry in this picture; and the "mission" of the Church. Indeed the Church, properly understood, *is* mission. If, as I have so frequently quoted from Whitehead, "a thing is what it does," then this last point is obvious. Unfortunately it is not always seen to be so.

Furthermore, the point of Dennis Nineham's remark about what God was "up to in Jesus Christ" needs to be reiterated. There is no sense in thinking or speaking of the Christian enterprise as if it occurred in a total vacuum. Neither is there any meaning in the event of Jesus Christ if it is taken, as it has been in some theologies, without continual reference to its consequences in succeeding history. The causal efficacy of any event is integral to that event. No action in nature, history or human experience is separable from what it has brought about, as if it stood in lonely splendor by itself. There are some who have sought to interpret the event of Jesus Christ in and of itself alone, perhaps with attention to its antecedents in Jewish faith and practice but without regard for what its occurrence has brought about. The Church, in the profound sense, is "what the event has brought about." Hence Nineham's remark is both relevant to our discussion and important for the proper grasp of the originative Christian fact which the apostolic witness communicates, the living tradition as a whole conveys, and contemporary Christian experience builds upon and expresses.

In the Pauline literature in the New Testament the Church is called "the Body of Christ." While this is not to be taken, as it has been taken by some, to be a biological image, it certainly is indicative of the way in which in primitive Christianity the community was understood to be integral to the event of Jesus Christ. Indeed, in Ephesians a post-Pauline writer speaks about Jesus Christ as with those who are his "members" in a relationship of head and body, so that he is able to act in and through them in a most intimate manner. So also in St. John's Gospel, where the image of "vine and branches" is used with much the same aim: the Church is the community of those who respond to the reality of Christ, as a branch is integral to the vine of which it forms a part. To put this in the language which we have adopted in this book, we may say that the Christian fellowship is to be interpreted as so much a part of the event of Jesus Christ in its wholeness that it is indeed the community of love in which the divine Love-in-act (God as Christians must understand God), which was enacted in the humanity of the central figure (from whom that community takes its origin), is both present and active. In consequence to "belong" truly to the Church *is* to be empowered to live in love, both with other humans and also in and with God focally disclosed and released in the originative event.

Now if this is in truth the nature of the Christian Church, it is no incidental or accidental accompaniment of the faith, but an essential aspect of that faith. To put it all too briefly, to be a Christian is to be a churchman—not, of course, in the sense of merely nominal membership in a particular social group; but in the profound meaning of actually participating in the "social process" which has come into existence because of Jesus Christ, with the objective of continuing to make actual the action of God through that event in its speciality. To repeat Nineham's emphasis, this is what God was "up to": to bring into existence a communal expression of the divine loving, with its consequences, so that men and women down the ages will have the possibility to live "abundantly," as those who are to become lovers-in-the-making here and now in this concrete world of space and time.

But the fellowship is not only "militant here in earth," as the familiar phrase has it. It is also a community whose membership includes those who, in the past, have belonged to it and are now received into the divine life. In other words, the Church "triumphant in heaven" must be emphasized, as must the Church "expectant," when this latter is taken to include all who in any way have "looked for" or are still "looking towards" (for that is what "expectant" means) such reception by God into the divine existence, where they may abide forever in what Hartshorne and others have called the "infallible divine memory." So it is that we shall not do justice to the deepest meaning of the Church if we confine our attention to the contemporary and plainly visible society or societies which are usually meant when we use the word "church."

To speak of the Church properly we must also understand that despite all superficial appearances there is about it what have been called in traditional thought the "notes" of unity, holiness, catholicity and apostolicity. About each of these something must now be said, however briefly.

The Church is "one," not because it is obviously so at this present moment. Alas, this is not the case! The unity of the Christian fellowship is at the deepest level, in the loyalty of Christian people to the Lord whom they follow. If one may put it this way without succumbing to a gnostic fallacy, it is a "spiritual unity." "One fellowship we dwell in him, one Church above beneath," as the hymn phrases it. A common loyalty exists, in greater or lesser intensity, as men and women have responded and still respond to the action of God upon them in terms of the divine enactment in human existence seen in the originative event. The unity is not man-made or man-conditioned; it is a given unity and has to do with divine priority. Yet it must be expressed outwardly and visibly. One of the remarkable features of contemporary Christian thought and work is the earnest effort to achieve, through reunion of the various separated Christian groups, precisely such a manifest oneness: "that they all may be one," as Jesus Christ (in the Fourth Gospel) is said to be "one with the Father."

Again, the Church as holy is the fellowship called by God to be a divine agency in the world, not exclusively but representatively and focally. Holiness is not in the first instance a matter of moral rectitude. Rather it signifies belonging to God. The Jewish term for exactly such "belonging" was the Hebrew equivalent of our word holiness."

But there will be moral consequences as well, although that is putting it far too weakly. It is not so much ethical goodness which is the point here as it is the reflection in the life of the world of the sort of total devotion or dedication to the divine purpose as (for Christian faith) was the motif of the life of Jesus himself in "the days of his flesh." This is sanctity, not as separation from the world but as the living of life in the world in such a relationship with God as shall manifest the divine purity, concern, justice and self-giving. The Church is the place where such are to be seen, however blurred or marred by human imperfection and error. Once more it is the responsibility of those who are members of the community to strive for the outward manifestation of this holiness, not by their own effort alone but in response to the grace (or divine Love-in-action) which is available in the "social process" and characterizes the "stream of influence" which is that community.

The Church as catholic is to be interpreted in both of two ways. On the one hand, it has to do with the fellowship as an integrated whole, in which faith and worship and discipleship are intimately related. The word "catholic" comes from the Greek *kath'olou* whose basic meaning is precisely such integration and harmony. On the other hand, the catholicity of the Church has to do with its being for all people, at all times, and in all places. Thus it is not sectarian or narrow, with significance for only a few; it is universal or worldwide in its purpose and in its mission. Or, as nowadays it is often said, it is a matter of the *oekumene,* the worldwide mission and work which is proper for those who have been caught up into the "stream" and have been made active participants in the "process."

Finally, as apostolic, the Christian community is characterized, in the first place, by its maintaining the centrality of the witness given in the earliest days (in apostolic times) to the event of Jesus Christ, proclaiming what it believes to be true: that in this historical event there was indeed an enactment of the divine Love-in-act in genuinely human terms, wrought out under human conditions and with all the limitations as well as all the given opportunities for divine action on the human historical level. But the word "apostolic" also has the sense of "being sent," as were the first apostles, to testify to others about that which in Christian faith we believe to have been done in Jesus

Christ. It is this second sense of the word which brings us to speak
of the Church's *mission in the world*.

That mission has to do with more than witness alone. It has to
do with concrete activity which will show, in what is being done by
those "who profess and call themselves Christian," that God has both
disclosed the divine character and has also "let loose," through the
event of Jesus Christ, the power of Love, to the end that the things
of this world may be conformed to the intention with which God
is actively at work in the created order. As I have so often said in
this book, that purpose is, as Teilhard so admirably phrased it, nothing
other than a process of "amorization." The divine Love, with its
corollary in the divine concern for liberation and justice and deliverance
from all oppression, is both unfailing and indefatigable. The mission
of the Christian community is to proclaim this and to act in such
a fashion that it is more than a matter of words but is also and primarily
a matter of definite deeds that can affect the course of events in human
history and in the experience of men and women everywhere.

In that mission, every member of the Church has his or her part.
Hence there is a ministry which belongs to every member. What is
called the "priesthood of the laity" is, in fact, the ministering vocation
(so to say) which is entailed when the laity—the "people of God" or
ho laos tou theou in Greek, to use New Testament idiom—are brought
to recognize the vocation which is theirs. In another book, *The Ministry
of All Christians* (Morehouse-Barlow, Wilton, CT, 1983), I endeavored
to treat this in such a fashion that it may be seen that in the celebration
of sacraments, the proclamation of the gospel, the shepherding of
God's human children, in study and teaching, and above all in the
life of discipleship, the whole community is involved. The Good
Friday collect speaks of "every member of [the Church] in his [or
her] vocation and ministry"; this tells us that an authentic understanding of Christian "Church-appurtenance" is a matter of genuine
ministering in response to the divine vocation to be men and women
"in Christ."

Such an emphasis is the prerequisite for any sound discussion
of the specific ministry belonging to those who have been ordained
to "any office and administration" in the Church. There is no separation
of such persons from the wider ministry of all Christians; but there

is a distinction in that *somebody* properly designated is needed if the mission of the fellowship is to be carried out. That is to say, there is no ontological difference attaching to the ordained person; yet there is a difference in functional responsibility and labor. The day when we could speak intelligibly about *status* in respect to those who are ordained passed away when we came to see that ours is not a *static* world, in which one or another person might be separated from others and given a position which denied those others their genuine participation in the whole process of creation. In place of that erroneous—and as we now know, non-biblical—notion, there is possible a stress on functioning which is proper for this or that given person within the whole community of the faithful. This is why no ordained person can dare to speak of his (or her) celebration of the sacraments, as was often done. It is always a matter of the whole fellowship doing this celebration, but doing it through the agent designated to act on behalf of and as representative for the community itself.

We now return to the Christian Church as the "loving community." With the characteristics to which attention has been called and with the mission which is integral to the community—for the Church is mission—the Church is primarily that specific process in history where the love of God, released through the event of Jesus Christ, is made available to succeeding generations of men and women, who may enter into it by the sacrament of baptism and thus know "newness of life in Christ Jesus." In the fellowship they may find a significance for their lives; through it they may receive the refreshment and empowering which will strengthen them for discipleship; and in belonging to it they share in a common life where each of them is supported by others and where all of them discover that they count enormously in the working out of the divine purpose in the world.

This does not suggest that such life in love is available *only* in the fellowship called Christian. I have already emphasized that this cannot be the case if God is indeed the "boundless Love" which is disclosed in Jesus Christ. What is implied here is no such exclusivist or "imperialistic" claim. On the contrary, what is asserted is that the kind of life in love (made free from the lovelessness, loneliness, alienation and unacceptability which dogs human existence much if not all of the time) that marks the Christian community when it is showing itself for what it really is, is precisely what God is seeking to elicit and to make actual for all the sons and daughters of the human race. Wherever and however, elsewhere and otherwise, something of this sort is made possible for men and women, there God is equally operative. But as I have urged earlier, such general truths are likely to lack cutting-edge and to have little significance for most of us. What is needed is an *instance*, if you will a "classic instance," in which this general truth has a "local habitation and a name" and hence does not remain "an airy nothing." To speak in that fashion, and with that specificity, is not to attempt to dictate to God the terms by which divine concern is to be expressed. It is only to recognize that for us humans the way to truth is through given particulars which we need in order to grasp what is being said by such generalized phrases as "God is Love" and "God always acts lovingly."

A world view which makes it possible to talk in this fashion is necessary for our Christian faith, since all believing is done in some context. But such a world view is not sufficient to make the affirmation come home directly and relevantly to each one of us. This is where the stance of faith is required. Hence here as elsewhere we have to do with what St. Anselm was talking about when he spoke of *fides quarens intellectum*—faith seeking to find some rationale in terms of which it may be expressed coherently and consistently, with due regard for all human experience in its every range. In the Christian fellowship that faith is maintained; the task of the Christian thinker is to relate it, so far as possible, to the rest of human knowledge, so that men and women may come to a deeper awareness of what their existence implies and may be helped to "give a reason for the hope that is in them." Otherwise, it could be that faith becomes mere credulity, lacking significant context and even coming close to denying the wider activity of God in the creation.

When the Christian community of faith, worship and discipleship is understood along these lines, it is apparent that it is rightly called "the loving community" and that its existence is integral to the event of Jesus Christ, with its freeing of men and women *from* their wrongness—the lovelessness, loneliness, estrangement and alienation, and feeling of unacceptability—and its freeing of them *into and for* a life together. Again and again I have spoken of the "stream of influence" which is the consequence of the event of Christ; here, in the community where men and women may live in love together, that stream has a focal expression. In the beginning of this chapter I observed that the institutional, organized and hierarchical Church does not adequately manifest this which is its secret character and mission. As Archbishop William Temple used to say, it is part of the common Christian vocation to work and pray that "the Church may become the Church," realizing and expressing outwardly in the affairs of human life what is its genuine place in the divine intention. This is why Christian reunion is so important; a divided and broken Church is a scandal.

Furthermore, the relationship of the empirical Church to the kingdom of God, which is the divine sovereign rule in love, needs to be emphasized constantly. When Vatican II spoke of that kingdom or divine reign as "subsisting" in the Church, rather than "existing" in it or "identical" with it, the point was made. To think of the empirical community as itself *being* the kingdom is a horrifying instance of human pretention; and when that claim is made in an attitude of triumphalist or imperialist superiority, the result is nothing short of blasphemy. At the same time, however, we must avoid the fairly prevalent attitude that "church membership" is entirely incidental and has no real and necessary part and place in the Christian obedience. I believe that the sort of approach which has been advocated in this chapter can be of assistance because it rejects both of these extremes, simple and uncritical identification on the one hand and total indifference on the other.

To put the matter very simply, to be freed by the objective action of God in Jesus Christ, as this has been given response in the subjective faith of men and women down the ages, *is* to be brought into just such a communal life in which both personal and social existence have their place and in which, as Nineham said, God is indeed making available for his children "a community under the lordship of the Risen One, in which reconciliation with God himself and the power of a holy life become, at least potentially, a reality." But now we can omit "potentially" and substitute some other words, perhaps "initially and then increasingly," so that we dare affirm that this "holiness" (which is life in love under God who is love) is slowly but effectually being realized inwardly in human hearts and being manifested outwardly in human action for caring, just dealing, deliverance from oppression, and the fullness of life which in the Fourth Gospel Jesus is represented as saying was why he had been "sent into the world." To put this in Jewish idiom, which Jesus himself as a loyal Jew would have known and valued and used, the divine *chesed* (or faithful loving-mercy) has brought into existence a community where *shalom* (or peace and abundant life) is given to the men and women whom God loves and for whom God constantly acts in many different ways, at all times and in all places and for all people.

The chief rite in which the Christian community celebrates, acknowledges, and receives this divine gift is eucharistic participation. So the Catholic tradition has always said; so also and more and more in our own time the denominations springing from the sixteenth-century Reformation are coming to understand and stress. This is why it is appropriate for us to discuss the eucharist, with its several aspects and its central place in Christian discipleship. In that eucharistic action the freedom to love is decisively enacted; through its celebration men and women are incorporated, again and again, into the "stream of influence" which conveys to them both the loving-mercy of God and the power to respond to it in dedicated, committed and faithful living.

8

Eucharistic Worship

This chapter is an attempt to present the significance of the eucharist in the light of the conceptuality called Process Thought and with special reference to its place in human deliverance by God's love available in Jesus Christ. Because of its necessary brevity, it can claim only to be what on the continent nowadays is styled "programatic," with the hope that others may develop in more detail the several points which will be suggested.

Before coming to the consideration of the eucharist itself, it will be useful to repeat in a few words the main emphases in the Process way of looking at things. In Britain (where this book is being written) not much attention has been given to Process Thought, although in North America, Latin America, Australasia, and more recently on the continent of Europe, many theologians, including Roman Catholics in increasing number, have adopted it. Anglicans in particular have been slow to recognize its value, although its two founding fathers, Alfred North Whitehead and Charles Hartshorne, were sons of priests—of the Church of England in Whitehead's case and of the American Episcopal Church in Hartshorne's. I set down here once again, to refresh our minds, main emphases in Process Thought.

For Process Thought, the world is marked by process or becoming; it is not a "chain of being," in Lovejoy's phrase. But "process" is not to be identified with "progress," for although everything is in movement or change, this is not necessarily or always for the better. Process Thought sees the world as made up of "energy-events," but not of things or substances. It is a societal or organismic world, in which everything influences and affects everything else. Furthermore, it is a world in which there is feeling or grasping ("prehension") through which past events enter into present experience and provide material for decision. Such decision or choice runs through the whole creation, implying a degree of freedom which at some levels is minimal but at others (including human existence) is vividly experienced. In this world there is both continuity and the emergence of genuine novelty, so that newness is as much a reality as regularity. Every event in the world has a di-polar quality, with potentiality (what it may become) and actuality (what it is in fact becoming). But some events are of more "importance" (or have more significant value) than others, although every event has some degree of "importance." The more important ones are those which vividly sum up the past, are decisive in their present impact, and open up new possibilities in the future; hence they are distinctively revelatory of what is going on in the world at large. Finally, the world is more influenced by persuasion than by coercion, despite the presence of much that we recognize would seem to contradict this interpretation.

These general principles are drawn from our own human self-awareness and from observation of what is around us. They are principles which may be generalized to apply to the entire creation. And if there is a reality which is worshipful, dependable and unsurpassable by anything not itself (in other words, if God exists), that divine reality is not the supreme exception but "the chief exemplification" (as Whitehead said) of these principles. Such is the assertion of Process Thought, with its verification (so far as may be) in experience and observation.

There can be no doubt that in the mainstream of Christianity, which in Process idiom may properly be called a "social process" (that is, a living tradition), the eucharist is the chief act of worship and has become a specially vivid expression of what the entire Christian view of the world enterprise asserts. If "the man from Mars" were to visit earth, he could be shown a Christian congregation engaged in eucharistic worship and told that this is what Christianity *really is:* the adoration and service of God decisively disclosed and released in the event of Christ, with response in faith and the enabling of the participants to share a life in love and a profound concern for the righteousness and justice which are both dependent upon and the consequence of love. The origins of the eucharist are not our interest here. Suffice it to say that from earliest days, according to the apostolic witness (upon which we depend for our knowledge of the formative period of the Christian tradition), eucharistic celebration has been seen as obedience to the desire, and perhaps even to the command, of Jesus at the Last Supper when he broke bread and shared the cup with his immediate followers. The eucharist has been "done" by Christian people down the centuries, sometimes in great simplicity and sometimes in grandeur and beauty; it has been their chief way of realizing the present activity of God in Christ and their opportunity to receive the grace ("divine favor and love") of the Lord whom they accept as God's signal action in human affairs.

In the Christian tradition the eucharist has been interpreted as including a memorial, an oblation or offering, a "presence" of the Lord, communion, the bestowal of "benefits," and mission. I shall discuss each of these, trying to show how the Process conceptuality can illuminate them and in particular illuminate our redemption as this is "summed up" (in Aquinas' words) in eucharistic action. In one very practical sense, this sort of approach leaves things as they were. It is not absolutely novel nor does it reject out-of-hand the traditional assertions about eucharistic worship. But it provides a different perspective and it may assist us in discerning more satisfactorily what those assertions, phrased of course in a different idiom, were attempting to get at.

1. *Memorial.* This does not mean pious reverie or merely a mental recollection of what happened in the event of Jesus Christ. "The continual remembrance of the sacrifice of the death of Christ," in the language of the Book of Common Prayer, becomes in Christian faith and through eucharistic action a present reality. Just as in the Jewish *seder* the deliverance of the Jewish people from Egyptian captivity is annually reenacted so that what might have been merely an occurrence in the dead past becomes a living experience in the present moment, so also the eucharist is anamnesis. In the idiom of Process Thought those past originative events are newly prehended or grasped

and are made effectual in the experience of men and women today. As the Anglican-Roman Catholic International Commission has recently defined this in its remarkable agreed *Report*, "the once-for-all event of salvation becomes effective in the present through the action of the Holy Spirit" (p. 19). Nor is it only the Cross which is thus made present; it is the total life of Christ, brought to its climax on Calvary with Easter following, since (as I have already quoted) *tota vita Christi misterium crucis* ("the whole life of Christ is the mystery of the Cross"), in words that medieval theologians were wont to use.

Now in Process thinking, the past is always seen as causally efficacious in the present. Its influence and its affect are inescapable. It is "remembered" in much more than a mental fashion. So eucharistic "memorial" is not an anomaly which is entirely unparalleled in human experience or in the world process. In that action, as in all events or occasions, the past is brought into the immediacy of present experience, asking for decision and making a difference. The originating event of Christ becomes "alive today," when the Christian community reenacts what its Lord is believed to have done at the Last Supper.

2. *Oblation.* This is the sacrificial aspect of the eucharist. It is not that *we* offer Christ once again but that *he* incorporates us into his own oblation to the Father. Of course no past event can be simply repeated. A Process understanding is especially insistent upon the specificity and speciality of every event; each has its own "uniqueness," which means that it is definitively itself, not repeatable also not lost in some vague generality.

On the part of the worshipers, to use again words from the International Commission, there is "a sacrifice of praise and thanksgiving" for what has been accomplished in the "one, historical, unrepeatable sacrifice, offered once for all by Christ and accepted once for all by the Father." Yet "in the celebration of the memorial Christ unites his people unto himself so that the Church enters into the movement of his self-offering. . . . The Church in celebrating the Eucharist gives thanks for the gift of Christ's sacrifice and identifies itself with the will of Christ who has offered himself to the Father on behalf of all mankind" (*ibid.*, p. 20). Since it is the "the whole Christ," the *totus Christus* (in the phrase of St. Thomas Aquinas), that is here offered to the Father, there is available a sharing by the faithful Christian community in what God has done in the whole of Christ's human life among us.

The Process perspective is again helpful at this point, since in that conceptuality every event has its own speciality and can never be duplicated, but at the same time, through the efficacy of a past event in the present moment, there can be a real participation in its "once-for-all" quality. It is not lost or forgotten, but is experienced as actively efficacious in succeeding events and therefore produces consequences in which those later events necessarily share. So the community which "remembers Christ" is caught up into and participates in what was accomplished in the past. By letting itself be identified with that past-made-present, the Christian fellowship is enabled to serve as an instrument for the divine purpose of liberation operative in the originating moment. The way to such participation and activity is through a response of gratitude, praise, readiness and desire for discipleship. In Process idiom, the past now-made-present "matters" enormously. Its consequences are "a stream of influence" which works itself out as men and women are grasped by it and opened to its power. (I have used here again Whiteheadian words in order to make the point. He meant them in a general sense but I am using them with specific reference to the Christian act of worship.)

3. *Presentness.* I prefer this word to "presence" because it emphasizes the personal quality of the coming of Christ to his people in the eucharistic action. I also prefer it because it does not suggest a more static view of *thereness*, but in the context puts the stress on an activity which includes necessarily an awareness of the one who is there active. It also may help us to avoid the difficult (and to us insoluble) question of the "how" of that eucharistic coming, while it makes impossible any talk about *location* in the total action. Aquinas rightly said that Christ is not in the eucharist *sicut in loco* ("as if in a place"). Process thought provides a way of affirming the "real activity" which there occurs without getting us bogged down in problems of the mode of "real presence." The International Commission says that "the real presence can only be understood *in the context of the redemptive activity* whereby [Christ] gives himself and in himself reconciliation, peace, and life, to his own" (*ibid.*, p. 14, my italics). That there is

a presentness of saving activity of the Lord in the eucharistic action is a given fact of Christian experience. In it the believer is renewed in his or her being freed to live in love.

That given fact can be seen in Process terms as a way in which we are both prehended and grasped by, and ourselves can prehend and grasp, an act which has objectively been done. It is *really* done (hence objective); it is known in that its being done is experienced and has its genuine result (hence subjective). Our total selves respond to its impact upon us; thus our existence is given a point and meaning which otherwise would not be available. In the vital recall which is eucharistic "memory," the objective reality of liberating divine action in and through Christ is effectively available (hence "present") for the subjective response of those who "assist at" the celebration. This is not in terms of a static presence but in terms of a "doing" in human experience in the event of Christ which is also an instance of the "going-on" of God in his ways of working actively in the creation.

4. *Communion.* Through participation in the eucharist a deepened relationship is established both between God, enacted in Christ, and God's human children *and* among those children one with another. Brought into communion with God they share in a fellowship which is much more "real" than ordinary and inevitably more superficial human contacts. Because their Lord is a signal focus of divine activity ("the divinity of Christ") and also the "proper Man" who fulfills human possibility ("the humanity of Christ") with all the limitations and conditions inevitable in creaturely existence, the communion with *God* in Christ is at the same time communion with *other humans* in that same Christ.

In Process Thought, the societal nature of all existence, divine as well as human, is strongly emphasized. Nobody lives to and for himself or herself; we all share in a "bundle of life," as an Old Testament text puts it. Thus to be drawn into Christ's presentness through a vivid and effectual activity is to be incorporated thereby into his oblation once offered. He is "remembered" as a living reality and not as a dead hero from the past. All this can be seen in Process terms as a relationship which so firmly unites those who participate, and is so much a divine gift rather than a mere human achievement, that it may rightly be called "the fellowship of the Holy Spirit." It is not of our devising but of God's giving. It is the consequence of what God has "determined, dared, and done" in the originating event of the Christian social process and hence it has an enduring quality which is renewed every time that eucharistic participation takes place. Using an Augustinian idiom, Dom Gregory Dix once said that "we receive the Body of Christ so that we may become the Body of Christ." He might be said almost to have spoken as a Process thinker—although those of us who knew him can imagine the horror with which he would have heard that comment!

5. *Benefits*. Aquinas asserted that the chief benefit of eucharistic participation is "unity in Christ." That unity has been noted in the preceding discussion. But here I add that the unity which is here in view is "unity in love"—and Aquinas also emphasized this. The grace which the Holy Spirit gives is "the love of God in action." That last phrase is from Kenneth Kirk who, in his *Vision of God*, argued convincingly that grace is no "thing" but is rather the divine working in all its personal quality. And N. P. Williams, in his now almost forgotten little book *The Grace of God*, urged that we must rethink the whole concept of grace in order to give due place to the personal and personalizing aspect of all God's working with his human children. Hence the grace which is given in the eucharist to establish "unity in Christ," which is by that very fact "unity in love," is no *thing*. It is nothing other than the divine Love-in-act, disclosed *as* active in the event of Christ and liberating and savingly released through him. Thus those who respond are "accepted in the Beloved" and empowered for Christian living. This is unity *par excellence*, established in the communion of men and women with Christ and with one another.

Again, Process thinking can be of help. Whitehead once told a research student (Nels Ferrè) that in his view a good definition of reality would be: "What matters and has consequences." The eucharist is an action which *matters*. It is both important and effectual. And *it has consequences:* its result is precisely the "stream of influence" which provides a sharing in the divine life-in-love so that those who participate are made sharers also in a unity which is enduring, indeed everlasting, and not merely ephemeral or sporadic. Every energy-event, every occasion, every instance of becoming, matters somewhat. They can never be lost or forgotten but have their inevitable result both for the world and in God. For Christian faith this event of Christ, as here "remembered" in eucharistic action, matters supremely. Its consequences are such that we are given both a context for and a renewing share in the Christ who is both *from* God and *with* us humans, for our being made free to live humanly in the loving relationship which gives true wholeness.

6. *Mission.* The last words of the old Latin mass were: *Ite, missa est,* "Go out now, you are being *sent.*" In the English Alternative Service Book much the same thing may be said by the celebrant or deacon at the conclusion of the eucharist; and in that Book's version of the rite there is also a splendid prayer: "Send us out in the power of your Holy Spirit to live and work to your praise and glory." Unless the participation of Christian people in eucharistic celebration leads to a continuing life in love and a dedicated action for God's service and "to his praise and glory," it has been short-circuited. Emil Brunner remarked in a quite different connection that "God's grace becomes our task." Those who have been participants in the eucharist are to show themselves, by life and conduct, to be in fact "eucharistic people," whose daily existence will be the consequence and reflection of that eucharistic worship. They are meant to become personal instrumental agents for the love of God enacted in Jesus Christ and still active in the world, because that same Christ is now "risen from among the dead" and "let loose into the world" (as is well said in John Masefield's play *The Trial of Jesus*) to bring more of that divine Love, with the justice which it entails, to more people, at more times, in more places and in more ways.

Process Thought speaks insistently of the inevitable consequences of what has been accomplished or achieved in the world. These consequences are received by God into the divine life; they make a difference to God in the ways of adapting divine love to and working in the ongoing "creative advance." They are also poured back into the creation for its further advance. This general principle is given vivid and specific expression for the Christian believer when it is used to interpret Jesus Christ. In the originating event, remembered and made effectually present in eucharistic celebration, with its offering to God, its establishment of enduring fellowship, and its engracing of those who have responded to it, *something happens.* Christ's "pilgrim people" are now enabled to share in an actualizing of their life in love, because their existence is now realized as grounded in *divine* Love and renewed by their eucharistic sharing. *They* are different, too. Their freedom to love has been effectively manifested and specifically communicated.

There is another point, never to be forgotten. In Christian understanding, the eucharist has always been seen as having an "eschatological aspect." The International Commission speaks about this: "The Lord who . . . comes to his people in the power of the Holy Spirit is the Lord of Glory. In the eucharistic celebration we anticipate the joys of "the age to come." By the transforming action of the Spirit of God, earthly bread and wine become the heavenly manna and the new wine, the eschatological banquet for the new man: elements of the first creation become pledges and first fruits of the new heaven and the new earth" (*ibid.*, p. 16). Thus we can properly say that the eucharist anticipates, or gives us a preliminary share in, the life of the kingdom of God.

That kingdom is nothing other than God's sovereign rule in love and justice. It is not yet known to us in its fullness; it can never be known to us in that fullness so long as we are pilgrims and wayfarers in this finite world. But in God it is ever-present. In the eucharist we have been given to know, as it were, "a little bit of heaven" made available to us here and now in our earthly pilgrimage. The biblical (and poetical) way of saying this is through talk of a "second coming"— we celebrate the eucharist "until he come."

Once more, Process Thought comes to our aid. In the very life of God who (in Whitehead's phrase) is "the Harmony of harmonies," all the good which is accomplished in the world is treasured, ordered and used, not for some supposed divine self-exalting "contentment" but for the furthering of loving and righteous purposes. This affirmation requires of us a certain "de-mythologization" of the traditional eschatological view. Thus to "de-mythologize" is in no sense to make that view irrelevant or unimportant. On the contrary, it is to give it a significance which relates it to any and every event in creation. There is no "neo-Platonic" escape into a static realm of ideals. This reconception also delivers us from literalistic interpretation of the biblical teaching. To speak in this different fashion about the eschatological perspective, with a special concern for the existential demands that it makes, is to urge that the energizing of divine Love is inexhaustible; and it is to say that human action, thus energized, can take place precisely because it is informed by the vision of the divine reality ceaselessly at work to establish a reign of love with justice. Anything that contributes to that end is received by and given place in God's life. It is never lost or forgotten, because it is indeed received into God and employed by God in the never-failing activity of "amorization." Therefore to be "in heaven" is not to be removed *from* the world but is to know the profound reality of divine working *in* the world. It is to be opened to employment by the gracious God who ceaselessly works out his purpose in the creation.

In this context, resurrection is a way of saying in biblical (and again poetical) idiom, two things integral to Christian faith. First, through the total event of Jesus Christ and then by sharing in that event, all those who are members of Christ are seen as indeed received by God. Second, what has been achieved humanly speaking is therefore understood in faith to be "unlosable"; it has made a genuine difference and it has had its consequences. In the Process perspective nothing is lost which can be saved; even evil can be transformed into an occasion for good, of which once again the Good Friday—Easter Day story is the Christian paradigm. The eucharist as eschatological in orientation makes this very plain.

In what way does a Process interpretation differ from other ways of seeing the eucharist? In one respect, as I said at the beginning of this chapter, it does not differ very much. All the main traditional emphases are retained. What it does provide is a way of setting the eucharistic action (and as I have argued other aspects of Christian faith, worship and practice, too) in a different context. Above all, because it is insistent on *activity*, seeing that "a thing *is* what it *does*" (as I have so often quoted from Whitehead), a Process interpretation can deliver us from many problems, such as those of "presence" as a thing; of how we can see eucharistic anamnesis; and of the meaning of the eschatological aspect of eucharistic action.

I have already said several times that I should be the last person in the world to say that the Process way is final or absolute. Are humans ever given such an assurance? Yet what I do urge is that it is *a* way, and to many of us a highly illuminating and even a compelling way, to make sense of insights and affirmations that have so consistently been found in the living tradition or social process we call the historical Christian community. Process Thought is no substitute for these insights and affirmations. But it can be used by responsible Christian thinkers in a fashion that enables us to say the old things in a new manner, as well as to say new things which (dare I suggest it?) the Holy Spirit may be teaching us in our own day. That is no unimportant service. Above all, it is invaluable in our attempt to interpret the eucharist as an expression of God's freeing of his children to live and act in love; hence of their knowing redemption and deliverance.

The eucharist is a social action in which persons are participants. But it does not stand alone. There is also the practice of prayer, as an enterprise in which each man and woman who "professes and calls" himself or herself after the Christian name, may engage and should engage. For it is necessary that human existence, which is both a matter of personal movement towards God's image *and* also a societal affair in which each helps others and others help each, shall have its proper double manifestation. That is why in the next chapter we shall turn to those occasions in which God's children give their personal and prayerful "attention" to God in the conscious effort to make real for themselves God's activity on their behalf.

9

Christian Praying Today: Attention to the Divine Love

The subject of this chapter is prayer in the context of Christian life as delivered by God from wrongness and hence freed to love. But the title which I have given it makes the subject much more precise; and before we proceed further I wish to say something about each of the three words in that title.

The noun is "praying" and it is modified by the adjective "Christian" and the adverb "today." What do I intend by the noun "praying"? Why am I using the adverb "today"?

To speak of "praying" is to speak of the actual doing of prayer. If we were going to talk about "prayer" in an abstract sense, defining it as if it were a thing, we would not really be considering what is going on when men and women engage in it. We would be concerned with a subject that happens to interest us, as it were, from the position of a spectator who has noticed that a large number of people appear to think that on the whole it is a good thing. But engagement in prayer, the actual doing of it, need not then be in our minds. We are not concerned here with prayer as a thing, but with the activity of "praying," in which men and women do something that they believe to be highly important and even essential for them.

What then is it that they do when they are praying? Briefly, we can say that they seek to relate themselves, in one way or another, with a loving superhuman reality or power, upon which they are dependent and to which they believe they may turn consciously from time to time, giving that superhuman reality or power their full attention. They may ask or intercede; they may worship and adore; they may confess and give thanks. But in all these, they are doing something which in their belief relates them to the whatever-it-is that they would call divine or holy or sacred—in the common religious word, to God, who has "delivered" them from wrongness to rightness.

But the kind of praying with which we are here concerned is not an activity without context and presuppositions. We are thinking about *Christian* praying; hence the adjective becomes significant. To say that anything is "Christian" is to say that it belongs to a long historic tradition to which the one who prays is dedicated or loyal. To put it that way is to imply that there is a real connection with an event in the field of human history, an event to which we give the name of "Jesus Christ." That event is focused in someone who lived centuries ago in our world as one of us, but who is also someone who, for the historic tradition, is not forgotten or merely of antiquarian interest. The event is of contemporary importance. Why is this?

The answer is simply that for the historic Christian tradition this event has done three things. It has *disclosed* the nature of the superhuman reality or power with which one seeks to be related in praying; it has *made a difference* to God and to the world, so that things are not the same as they would have been if the event had never taken place; and it has *released into the world* a particular kind of "spirit" that brings freedom, while that same spirit is understood to be an abiding fact in the God to whom praying is directed. In other words, the historic tradition to which the praying person belongs says that God was disclosed or revealed or expressed in human terms in Jesus Christ.

In Jesus Christ something happened which has given to men and women awareness of a specific relationship to God which was not evisaged or at least not so fully grasped before the event took place. In Jesus Christ the members of the living Christian tradition have received their human freedom by the action of the Spirit (and now I put the "s" in upper class, for this is the Spirit of Jesus Christ himself), by which action they are assured that in God, with whom they are relating themselves in their praying, the reality of Jesus Christ is an abiding reality. This last aspect of the event is what they are getting at when they speak, as Christians have done for two thousand years, of the resurrection of Jesus Christ from the dead.

How and what went on in praying in earlier times is of importance for us *today* because we are linked with earlier generations through our belonging with those ancestors in faith to an ongoing "social process" of which we are the contemporary representatives. This is indeed true. Yet it is also true that men and women today have their own interests, concerns, needs and defects. Furthermore, they have new ways of thinking about and interpreting their world and hence have a different conception of things-at-large than did their forebearers. Any treatment of praying which will make much sense for men and women who live now and pray now must reckon with those differences, both of concern and of thought. If we look at God-world-human existence in our own modern way, taught this not only by our inherited faith but also by the circumstances in which we today hold that faith, we shall doubtless speak about the activity of prayer in a way that is not identical with (although it is certainly in genuine continuity with) what our ancestors in that faith understood their praying to be and how in their time they engaged in that activity. Only those who fail to see that "new occasions teach new duties," and that we cannot return to an earlier age that we may esteem but do not inhabit, will deny what has just been said. It is with our praying *today*, specifically with *Christian* praying and with the activity of *praying* as an inescapable element in Christian discipleship that we are concerned.

We humans are creatures who have emerged from and are part of a world which is not static, inert, immovable, changeless. It is a world which is characterized by process, in which there is both a continuity of pattern and the appearance of genuinely new things— or as I should prefer to say, of novel "events" or "happenings." Indeed, the world is made up of such events, which are foci of energy and which have their subjective side in that they are also centers of experience. Such experience is not always or necessarily conscious; it may well be a feeling that is vague and ill-defined but is nonetheless a present fact. Again in our world there is a profound kind of interrelationship so that everything affects and is affected by everything else. There is also a genuine freedom for decision, sometimes made with keen awareness and sometimes found simply in what is often called a "reaction" to influences or pressures. These decisions or "cuttings-off" have their consequences in later moments. Finally there is the attracting or luring or persuading which we have found to be much more effectual in the long run than the exercise of sheer force. In this world men and women know that they too share in these several aspects of existence. They are not fixed and static; they are moving towards or away from possible goals. Like everything else in the world, they are each of them instances of "becoming"; and because of the societal nature of that world they are also instances of "belonging," in greater or lesser intensity of awareness. They make their choices, whether these are big ones or little ones; and their choices have their results, for which the agents know themselves responsible. They are sometimes vividly conscious of such responsibility but often are only dimly aware of it. And they live in terms of response made to invitations, suggestions, solicitations or lures, which produce genuine consequences that are more enduring than responses made to coercive power at work upon them.

It is in this sort of world, and by this sort of person, that praying today takes place. But people do not feel they are praying in a vacuum; their praying is the urge and desire to relate oneself to, and establish some kind of contact or association with, that which, or the one who, is the chief creative and receptive agency in the world at large. This agency is usually perceived in a personal fashion. It is more like our being related to and associated with another person than like a relationship with an object such as a stone or a planet or some merely forceful thing. In other words, praying has to do with what religion calls God. The praying man or woman seeks to have a genuine contact or communion with the divine reality, which inevitably is thought about in terms drawn from human experience, since it is only from that experience that we can derive our concepts, make our pictures, or shape our models.

Christian praying, like Christian living, is essentially theocentric; it is centered on the reality of God. But what kind of God is it that we are talking about? How do we picture God? What model have we in mind when we use that three-letter vocable? I am afraid that a good deal of what is taken to be geniunely Christian is in fact nothing of the sort when it comes to our picture or model for God. Let me explain.

I have frequently quoted in this book from Alfred North White-head, the English philosopher who ended his days in the United States and who is for some of us the most important philosophical influence on our thinking. He was the "founding father" of the way of seeing the world and everything in it which has come to be called (not too happily, as I have said) "Process Thought." With the use of his general world view, we have been seeking in this book what might be styled a "re-conception" of Christian ideas, so that they will make room for the dynamic, processive, interrelational or societal interpretation of "things," which Whitehead so strongly urged and which best represents the truth as far as we can know it.

One of Whitehead's major concerns was to find a way of under-standing what is meant by God—a way that would not reflect older notions of an "imperial Caesar" nor a "metaphysical principle" nor a "ruthless moralist," but would center everything on what he called the "brief Galilean vision"—the event of Jesus Christ. There, in that event, he said, we are given a "disclosure in act" of what Plato and others discerned as "theory": that God is sheer Love, influencing and affecting the world and also influenced and affected *by* the world, so that what goes on in the world makes a real difference to God. To say and think that God is absolutely immutable, unaffected, self-contained, and entirely self-sufficient, is to subscribe to what Professor Charles Hartshorne, the American expositor of Whitehead's views, has styled the "classical conception of God." To speak in Whitehead's manner about God as related to and affected by the creation is called by Hartshorne the "neo-classical conception." In the present book I am assuming its validity.

What has just been said is highly relevant when we come to con-sider *Christian* praying; I emphasize the adjective because I wish to stress that whatever may be thought of other ideas of prayer, the Chris-tian one has its distinctive quality. A Christian is, or ought to be, pray-ing to God as decisively and focally disclosed in the event of Christ; and that means that his or her praying will reflect faith in God as redemptive Love-in-act, not as sheer power or abstract principle or moral dictator. Inevitably this Christian sort of praying will be a matter of loving relationship; yet it will also be filled with awe and wonder and the sense of mystery appropriate to the holiness of the cosmic Lover.

Some fifteen and more years ago the American Process theologian Schubert Ogden was speaking at a student conference on "The Credibility of God" held at a college in Ohio. In response to a question from a student about praying he said this: "It [is assumed] that on the classical conception of God you can somehow make sense out of prayer. . . . I flatly reject that assumption. . . . How can you pray to the classical Absolute to whom nothing makes any difference? I think that is one of the skeletons in the closet of classical theism. It kept summoning men to pray to a God to whom, in principle, prayer like everything else could make no difference whatsoever. [But] what would prayer mean within the neo-classical frame of reference? I should say that the Christian . . . has to look upon the question of prayer as he looks upon everything else—in the light of Jesus Christ. That's the reason Christian prayers always end with such phrases as "in the name of Jesus Christ" or "through Jesus Christ our Lord" or something like that. Thus all Christian prayer is . . . mediated by what the Christian believes to be the decisive revelation of God. But notice how all Christian prayers begin with phrases something like this, "Almighty and most merciful Father." Now, one thing you don't have to do to an almighty and most merciful Father is tell him things he doesn't know about. You don't have to inform him about matters concerning which he is ignorant. Furthermore, you don't have to twist his arm to do for you what he is not otherwise disposed to do. . . . The question is, What is prayer? What really goes on here? What is happening? It seems to me that what the Christian says is happening is that I as a person am now appropriating as my own and speaking back to God the word which he has addressed to me in and through the witness of the Church and in and through the actual life, existence, needs and possibilities of myself and my neighbor. . . . Prayer is the means of grace whereby I appropriate as my own [the] claim of God on my life. I would add that prayer is significant and meaningful at all only because it does make a difference to God, even as everything else does. . . . Luther and Augustine [said] long before [modern neo-classical theologians] that we do not pray to instruct God, but to instruct ourselves." (*The Credibility of "God"* Muskingum College, Ohio, 1967, p. 54-55.)

I have made this lengthy quotation not only because it is relevant to what has been argued in this book about deity, but also because it is useful to us in understanding that genuine praying is possible, rather than praying as a merely "Pickwickian" exercise, only when the picture of God is such that the praying has to do with a responsive deity; that is, with One who is affected by what is going on in the creation and by what men and women achieve or fail to achieve. This mutuality is to be seen above all in the activity of seeking a conscious relationship with God.

In a world such as that which we know today, with a God who is pictured in terms of sheer Love-in-act, and with the reality of deliverance into human freedom to love through what God has done in Jesus Christ, praying is no irrelevant exercise. God is always and everywhere actively present in such a world. Thus there can be no meaning in talk of God's "intrusion" into it, as if from somewhere "outside" it God "came" into the creation. Talk of "intrusion" is not simply an unfortunate way of talking about what I prefer to describe as "new initiatives" by the living God, who preserves continuities but also does "new things" (and that is ultimately why there are "novelties" in the world). That talk usually presupposes the "classical theism" that thinks of God as immutable, impassible, and without essential relationship to the creation. I contend with Professor Ogden that such a view of God makes genuine praying impossible or absurd. But with the "neo-classical" picture, where God and the world are mutually related in a give-and-take, the situation is entirely different and praying makes very good sense indeed.

It is *not* that we presuade God to do what God has hitherto been unwilling to do; it is *not* that we inform God of what previously God had not known; it is *not* that we engage in an "arm-twisting" of deity. Rather, it is that we *attend* to God who emancipates us to live truly human lives in love. As a matter of fact, one of the best definitions of prayer, from Dom Augustine Baker (a great master of praying in past Christian history) was precisely "the attentive presence of God." By means of such attention we give heed to, open ourselves for, and become responsive to the God whose loving activity (and hence loving "presentness") is *always* with us.

There is more than that, however. In thus attending and thus opening ourselves, we indicate our readiness to be God's "fellow workers," as St. Paul put it; "co-creators with God," as Whitehead so finely phrased it. In primitive religions, where God was taken to be sheer power, prayer was seen as a way in which (so it was thought) deity could be made to give us what we wanted or thought we wanted, having been forced by our praying to "change his mind." But in the Process concept of praying, God never "changes his mind," for that mind is unalterably and everlastingly love. Yet God *does* adapt the divine activity to men and women as, and where, they are, so that this is available to them precisely in their becoming aware of God, attentive to God, and responsive to God's loving and releasing activity within them and upon them and through them. Thus men and women can do exactly what Professor Ogden said: "appropriate as their own the claim of God on their lives." In doing this they are "speaking back to God" the word of love which first God has spoken to them in the event of Jesus Christ, known through the witness of the Church and given focus and point through "the actual life, existence, needs, and possibilities" of ourselves and of our fellow humans. Therefore prayer is not entirely separate and different from ordinary human experience; on the contrary it is that experience made fully conscious of what human existence signifies and what purpose it has.

Th Dean of Durham, Peter Baelz, has written a fine little book entitled *Does God Answer Prayer* (DLT, London, 1982), which may be enthusiastically recommended to anyone who is prepared to interpret praying along the lines which I have been suggesting. Dean Baelz insists that praying is to be sharply distinguished from "magical" exercises in which it is thought that somehow human beings can persuade God to do what otherwise God would never think of doing. On the contrary, Dean Baelz urges that *Christian* praying is precisely the seeking of a conscious relationship with the divine Love or Lover, learning to "wait upon" God and gladly willing to be available for God and for the fulfillment of God's purposes. The argument in his admirable book brings us to face fairly and squarely the sad truth that much which many devout people, and others too, of course, have assumed to be genuine praying is in truth nothing of the sort. It is far too much like the "arm-twisting" about which Ogden spoke.

We must consider therefore the purpose and meaning of the aspects of praying which are commonly called "petition" and "intercession." Before speaking of that, however, it ought to be stressed first that if what has been urged so far is correct, the elements in praying which are often called adoration, thanksgiving, praise, and the like, are primary; although on the other hand we can readily see that men and women are more likely to grow into an understanding of these primary elements only *after* they have started their praying in the more childlike fashion of "asking for things."

The right way of understanding petition and intercession is now apparent. It is natural and proper that in seeking to establish a relationship in which we "attend" to God, we shall be impelled to speak in word or thought about our own needs and those of others, as we happen to see them. Like any loving parent, God surely is prepared to "listen," as we may phrase it, to such statements of the supposed needs or desires of his (or her) children. Not that God can be persuaded to change the enduring purpose of love and the ceaseless action in love; to think that would be to assume that God is not Love-in-act, as we have seen God to be. Rather, our human expression of what we suppose we want or what we humans think we lack, by way of "things" both for ourselves and others, is part of the *self*, the total human existence, which is to be attentive to God and God's caring for us. As we grow in our praying, we shall come to understand that the old Prayer Book collect for XIV Trinity is correct as a prayer for "the increase of faith, hope, and charity" as the basic human needs. If, as that collect goes on to say, we wish to "obtain" what God "promises," it will be by just that "increase" that we shall become ready to receive those "promises." And what are they? From the Christian's grasp of God's disclosure and God's outpouring of love seen in the event of Jesus Christ, the "promises" can be only a greater freedom for loving and a greater capacity to live in love, under and with and for the Love that *is* God.

To quote here from a small book of my own published in 1974 (*Praying Today*, Grand Rapids, Mich., 1974): "For Christian faith Jesus is that One in whom the deepest and highest reality, divine Love, which is the mystery behind all things and the meaning of all things, is made decisively visible and tangible in a manhood that is our own and in terms that we can understand and grasp, and by which we can [also] be grasped and thus directed on the path of right and true human development . . . [Therefore prayer] is [our] desire to work with the purpose of Love; and so [praying] is our opening of self to that working" (p. 102). Thus we come slowly and perhaps painfully to understand the specifically theocentric nature of praying.

Yet our praying is not to be separated from the actual daily living which is in and with, under and for, divine Love or God. Time will be required if we are to learn this lesson; it is never easy to grasp the truth that to be a Christian is to exist *ad majorem dei gloriam*, for God's glory and not for our own self-centered and selfish interests. Of course the problem here is how to interpret that word "glory". For far too long it has been taken to picture God as sitting upon a heavenly throne exacting servile submission from lonely subjects and delighting in the divine self-sufficiency. We have already made plain that such a conception of deity bears no relationship to the genuinely Christian picture of deity. In that Christian picture God is affected by what happens in the world; God adapts the divine working to the condition and situation of human creatures; and God finds delight not in their regarding themselves as "worms" in the divine presence, but in their responding—in the fullest fashion possible for them—to the divine imperative of love and with the strengthening which divine loving provides. God is to be adored and thanked, praised and exalted, precisely as such Love-in-act.

For this reason, the proper setting for our praying is an increasing recognition of God's presence and action anywhere and everywhere in the creation, often in what may seen to us quite unlikely places— like a manger or a cross. To "abandon oneself" (as Père Jean de Caussade once put it) to that presence and that action in what de Caussade called the "sacrament of the present moment" is to live prayerfully; and our specific moments of praying are an invaluable focusing of our general intention and attitude, so far as we are able and just where we are. There is nothing magical about this; there is no arm-twisting here. On the contrary, there is the kind of receptivity or (if you will) passivity to God that is our highest human activity.

To understand what has now been said about praying is to begin to grasp the point of St. Paul's admonition that we should "pray without ceasing"; that *all* our life ought to be an openness to, a receptivity for, and an attentive awareness of God. On the other hand, to say what has been said is also to recognize the necessity for particular times and special occasions when what *ought to be* the case with our total existence becomes a concrete fact. Because we have other things in which we must engage, jobs to do, a house to care for, a child to tend, parents to look after, and so much else; because we live in this world with its constant demands, we need a concrete and specific fact with which we come to terms. That is why it is necessary and wise to establish a set time, place and opportunity for our praying. This is another case of general truths of pervasive requirements expressed in particular and specific instances. Otherwise it might very well be that to "pray without ceasing" could end up in our not praying at all.

The converse, however, can also be a danger. We may so stress the particular occasions, times and opportunities that we forget altogether that these are exactly that: special instances of what can and should become over the years and with more general responsible attention the leit motif of all our human existence. Here, as everywhere else in human experience, particularity and generality go together. The neglect of either is likely to imperil our understanding and impede our practice.

It seems to me that it is important to emphasize for many well-intentioned but not highly "religious" people the need for such particular occasions; while for the consciously religious the need is to stress the wider and more general aspect. The sad fact is that for a great many within the several Christian denominations, praying has become an approved but little practiced exercise, not least because there has been insufficient teaching given and almost no practical help provided in the matter. Hence they may turn to one or other of the cults which have come to us from the East. On the other hand, as I noted in one of the previous chapters in this book, men and women who do not belong to any religious group yet can and sometimes do show an awareness of the presence of the more-than-human which gets expressed in their devotion to music or poetry or art. This is an awareness perhaps not consciously understood but yet genuinely present also in their devotion to duty, their care for others, their dedication to great causes, or their sacrifice of self for this or that important human concern. Such people should be helped to grasp the fact that in a profound sense they are engaging in prayer.

I conclude this chapter by urging once more that *Christian praying today* is indeed a matter that requires us to think about its meaning. The strange thing is that once we have come to see praying as a relationship with God defined, disclosed and made available in the living Christian tradition whose focus is the event of Jesus Christ, we may also discover that in the living Christian tradition the great "masters" of praying have always talked and acted in a fashion similar to, if not identical with, what I have been saying. But this cannot be accepted simply and easily without bothering about our own particular contemporary concerns and needs. If we try to do that we shall turn the whole business into a mechanical repetition which has no direct relevance to ourselves. What is wanted is our own contemporary effort and activity. When we have made this a part of our existence, we shall learn that we are not alone but are part of a great company of Christian witnesses and participants in the great movement of life which is definitively Christian. Above all we need our own contemporary techniques and procedures in praying. Here we can be grateful to the many who have made it their business to show us how in our own day the ancient discipline of praying may be genuinely Christian *and* directly in touch with us in our present need as we accept our freedom in Christ to live in love.

All which brings us back to the main theme of this book: God's deliverance of human existence from its condition of lovelessness, with its accompanying loneliness and the sense of unacceptability. Somehow, in the event of Jesus Christ, countless millions of men and women have experienced freedom to live in love; they have been "freed to love." For that reason, their praying is primarily an expression of gratitude, not a pleading or petitioning even if these are often natural and proper ingredients in their address to their heavenly Father. Further, their day-by-day living is in agreement with this attitude of rejoicing in freedom.

In eucharistic worship, as we have said, there is available a participation in the divine Love brought near in Christ, so that humans who "live in him" and in whom he lives discover that they are knit together in a fellowship which is deeper and more enduring than ordinary human community can provide. "One company we dwell in him," says a familiar hymn; and that companionship is known, in varying intensity to be sure, when Christian people come together to assist at the offering of their "sacrifice of praise and thanksgiving." But the same awareness of "belonging," in a sense more profound than common human sociality is able to provide, also marks our praying in a more personal fashion. So it is that we say *"Our* Father," for Christian loyalty delivers us from the excessive individualism which so often mars our existence.

Whitehead's famous saying, that religion is what we "do with our solitariness," is in no way a denial of this "belonging." What he was concerned to affirm was something quite different; it was the truth that precisely in order to have genuine fellowship, each participant must of necessity have some glimpse of and some share in the "refreshment and companionship" which the divine Love alone can offer in an enduring and compelling way. Here we have to do with no "ant-hill" community where self-hood is denied and lost, but with a sociality which guarantees and enhances *each* participant precisely by providing for him or her a place in which each may make an appropriate contribution and from which each may receive due recognition as "a beloved child of God."

Truly Christian praying, then, has a social aspect quite as much as a personal one. This is inevitable because nobody who grasps the nature of Christian deliverance can venture to make claims about his or her "individual salvation." The popular remark, so often made in quite different contexts, that "we're all in this together" applies as much to our praying as to any other aspect of human existence. The Old Testament text already quoted, which speaks of our human existence as "a bundle of life," is to the point. Loneliness, which is very different from Whitehead's "solitariness," is overcome for us when we realize that we belong to what in the Christian tradition has been styled "the communion of saints." And that phrase, both in its original Greek as in Latin, includes our participation with "holy *ones*" and our participation in "holy *things.*" Thus the materiality of the creation, quite as much as immaterial values and attitudes and contacts, is guaranteed as valid and good. Not only so, but our responsibility for such materiality is emphasized. This is why, as we have already argued in a preceding chapter, nobody who calls himself or herself by the

the Christian name can avoid—can even want to avoid—a deep concern for justice, for economic and social and every kind of freedom, and a readiness to be associated with the struggle for such justice and freedom for every human, of every race and class and type.

Praying and living go together; and both find their supreme expression when the eucharist is celebrated. In assistance at that sacrament, we are permitted a glimpse of God and the world seen together in the *right* way, which is God's way of loving, with human response made freely and gladly.

Afterword

As I was putting some last touches on the preceding chapter I was visited by a young journalist who came to discuss with me a television program, of which he was to be director, which would present for a large national audience an account of contemporary religious thinking. He had been told that Process Theology was worth including in the program; hence his visit, since he had been informed that I had written much on the subject.

During the course of our conversation, this attractive young man (who seemed well informed on religious matters although he frankly confessed that he was no expert and could not even claim to be "especially devout") raised four questions which, he said had been suggested to him as the "basic difficulties about Process Theology." The questions were these: (1) Does not the Process conceptuality, when used for Christian purposes, deny omnipotence to God and make deity entirely finite and limited? (2) What place can Process thinking make for a deity who is (I use here my interviewer's own word) "external" to human experience and hence an "impossibility," in effect confining all talk about God to entirely "subjective human spirituality"? (3) How is it possible to pray to a God who is not completely "in control of the world," and if it *is* possible to do so, what use is prayer? (4) Would not a presentation of God in the terms which Process thinking suggests cause distress, discomfort and even pain to a great many devout church people?

Because of these questions which the journalist asked me, I have decided that this Afterword is necessary and may be useful for readers of this book, for I think that he stated what are the usual objections to the kind of theologizing which we have been discussing. I shall attempt to treat briefly each of the four questions just mentioned, although my basic concern is to see how they are relevant to the matter of redemption as freedom *from* what is wrong and freedom *for* a life marked by love and the active search for justice among and between humans.

The first question has to do with the notion of divine omnipotence. There can be no doubt that for a great many people God is thought to be absolutely all-powerful or (in the word from the creeds) "all-mighty." Yet in the history of Christian thought this assertion has never been made *tout court;* it has always been qualified in important respects. For example, in the scholastic theology of the Middle Ages, it was clearly said that God cannot do "the impossible"—like creating "a square circle." Furthermore, it was said that God cannot do that which is morally reprehensible or evil. To be sure there was a strand in later Calvinistic scholasticism which refused to make any significant qualifications of omnipotence and hence was prepared to represent deity (in a fashion not unlike that of William Occam in the Middle Ages) as so much "will" and so much the controller of all things that God could not be regarded as "bound" by anything save arbitrary decisions. Calvin himself did not take this view, either in *The Institutes* or in his many commentaries on books of the Bible; and the mainstream in the Christian theological tradition has consistently rejected it. In any event, it is worth observing that in the ancient Church God was called "sovereign governor of all things," rather than sheerly omnipotent. *Pantocrator* was the Greek word chosen for credal use and that word means precisely "sovereign governor."

In Process Theology this careful discrimination is continued and extended. God is said to be the possessor of all *conceivable* power, which means that God is seen as the chief but not the only entity to whom power belongs. The creatures *also* have power, of some sort and in some degree. Indeed it is only from our awareness of such creaturely power that we could possibly arrive at the notion that God has the *maximum* power possible in a world marked by creaturely freedom and accountability. If to say this is to talk about a "finite" or "limited" God, so be it! But the "finitude" is necessary if the creation is to have any such freedom and accountability as we experience it and ourselves to possess. The "limitation" of God, as Whitehead urged, is precisely the divine "goodness."

The second issue has to do with what my interviewer styled an "external" God and what I should wish to call an "objective" God. I have already said something about this in my brief consideration of the position of Don Cupitt, who has argued that the only deity about whom we may speak meaningfully is the "subjective spirituality" known to us in our aspirations, hopes, religious sensibility and moral concerns. As I said in that connection, no Process theologian has ever been prepared to take that line. In terms of a sound, if critical, realistic "epistemology" or theory of human knowledge, it is an impossible view. *All* our knowing, like *all* our human experience, has its setting in a world from which we have emerged as specifically human creatures. To think that our knowledge and our experience are entirely self-generated, with no reference beyond themselves and with no objective facts to which they are a response, is to indulge in an absurd anthropocentrism; what is more, it is to assume that this human thinking and experience appeared (like Topsy in the American folk tale) without antecedents and without context.

It may be claimed that of all contemporary efforts to "re-conceive" the doctrine of God, Process Theology is the one *most* insistent on this objectivity. It is correlative with, and the condition for, whatever may be the subjective response made in human experience and thought to a prior action of the world as a whole, and behind and through that world of the supreme reality which we call God.

What about prayer and answer to prayer in a Process way of doing theology? I have urged in the final chapter of this book that if God is "modeled" after the conventional pattern and taken to be absolutely unaffected by the creation, praying is indeed an absurd exercise. God "has it already *made*," as the saying goes. Nothing that humans may do will influence deity who has already determined exactly how things will go. The notion that such a God "answers" anybody or anything is so much a contradiction of that "model" that it can only be maintained by indulging in theological double talk. But as my quotation from Schubert Ogden was intended to show, a neo-classical (or

Process) portrayal of God both makes prayer a viable possibility and also insists that our praying "makes a difference" in the way things are going to go in the world. What it rules out is the idea that our praying is a "twisting of God's arm," as if deity had to be forced by human agents to do what otherwise would never be done and what in any event may very well be a contradiction of the divine love which is universal in its scope but always particular or specific in its application—in Whitehead's phrase, a "particular providence for particular occasions." Essentially prayer is "attention to God," openness to his lure, and readiness to serve as his instrumental agents in the effecting of the divine purpose; answer to prayer is not a denial of this, but the way in which we are led to see more profoundly what *is* that divine purpose and hence to "grow in grace" as its willing servants.

Finally we come to the feeling that if the Process kind of "re-conception" were adopted, a great many devout men and women would be seriously "disturbed" because in various ways that re-conception calls in question commonly accepted ideas about God and God's way in the world. My answer here is quite simple. What a good thing it would be if men and women were thus disturbed! For the situation is often that such people (and, alas, even their leaders among clergy and teachers) assume without any question that the *old* ideas are "absolute truth" and that suggestions for modification, in the light of the inescapable Christian criterion of God as Love-in-act and with honest recognition of new circumstances, as well as the acceptance of new knowledge, are almost by definition bound to be either heretical or "unChristian." I find it difficult to understand how people can think this way, above all how their responsible leaders can do so. Such nostalgia for the past is like all other ultra-conservative thought: it is nothing other than "fighting the grain of the universe." The spectacle of good people who are intent upon denying the living God who (in the words of the prophet Isaiah) "does new things" is distressing. Its continuation in our contemporary world is often taken to be an indication that the entire Christian enterprise is so out of touch with reality that it merits no attention and can win no support from those who refuse to indulge in backwoodmanship but are alert to the "signs of the times."

I end this Afterword, and hence this book, by affirming that Christianity is, as St. Augustine remarked in a quite different context, "ever old, yet ever new." For our main topic in this book, that double truth is shown very clearly in our effort to understand and make our own the perennial Christian insistence that in the event of Jesus and in the "stream of influence" which this event has "let loose" into the world, men and women today, as in ancient days, have been delivered from their captivity to false self-centeredness and liberated into the freedom to live as God's children in love and justice. They are brought in the Christian fellowship of love to respond with heart and soul and mind and strength to the prevenient loving activity of God for them and for their "wholeness."